Diversity as Liberation (II)
Introducing a New
Understanding of Diversity

THE HAMPTON PRESS COMMUNICATION SERIES
Communication Alternatives
Brenda Dervin, supervisory editor

The Reach of Dialogue: Confirmation, Voice and Community
   Rob Anderson, Kenneth N. Cissna, and Ronald C. Arnett (eds.)

Desert Storm and the Mass Media
   Bradley S. Greenberg and Walter Gantz (ed.)

Hearing Many Voices
   M.J. Hardman and Anita Taylor (eds.)

Theorizing Fandom: Fans, Subcultures, and Identity
   Cheryl Harris and Alison Alexander (eds.)

Responsible Communication: Ethical Issues in Business, Industry,
and the Professions
   James A. Jaksa and Michael S. Pritchard (eds.)

Communication and Trade: Essays in Honor of Meheroo Jussawalla
   Donald Lamberton (ed.)

Public Intimacies: Talk Show Participants and Tell-All TV
   Patricia Joyner Priest

Communication and Development: The Freirean Connection
   Michael Richards, Pradip N. Thomas, and Zaharom Nain (eds.)

Diversity as Liberation (II): Introducing a New Understanding
of Diversity
   Amardo Rodriguez

Nature Stories: Depictions of the Environment and Their Effects
   James Shanahan and Katherine McComas

The Gender Challenge to Media: Diverse Voices From the Field
   Elizabeth L. Toth and Linda Aldoory (eds.)

forthcoming

An Arsenal for Democracy: Media Accountability Systems
   Claude-Jean Bertrand (ed.)

U.S. Glasnost: Missing Political Themes in U.S. Media Discourse
   Johan Galtung and Richard Vincent

Diversity as Liberation (II)
Introducing a New
Understanding of Diversity

Amardo Rodriguez
Syracuse University

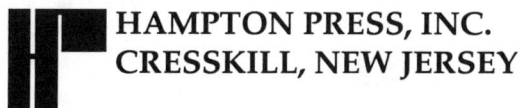
HAMPTON PRESS, INC.
CRESSKILL, NEW JERSEY

Printed in the United States of America.

Library of Congress Cataloging-in-Publication Data

Rodriguez, Amardo.
    Diversity as liberation (II) : introducing a new understanding of
    diversity / Amardo Rodriguez.
       p.cm. -- (Communication alternatives)
    Includes bibliographical references and index.
    ISBN 1-57273-354-3 -- ISBN 1-57273-355-1
      1. Pluralism (Social sciences) 2. Pluralism (Social sciences)--United
States. 3. Multiculturalism. 4. Multiculturalism--United States. I. Title.
II. Series

HM1271 .R63 2002
305.8'00973--dc21

                       2002022795

Hampton Press, Inc.
23 Broadway
Cresskill, NJ 07626

The sharing of joy, whether physical, emotional, psychic, or intellectual, forms a bridge between the sharers which can be the basis for understanding much of what is not shared between them, and lessens the threat of their difference.
Audre Lorde

To Joshua and Jordan
With the deepest of love

Contents

Acknowledgments

I will always be eternally grateful to Joy for the many sacrifices she made so I could bring this project to completion. It was by no means my aim to ask so much of a human being. Yet this project is personal to both of us. We want our children to be released from the many fears of diversity. I am glad that Brenda Dervin believed in the potential of the project. I must express my deepest thanks to two anonymous reviewers who were extremely supportive of the project and made many solid recommendations. I would also like to thank Stacy Seibert for the kind words of support and encouragement.

Prologue

This book is about diversity, liberation, and being human. It forwards a different understanding of diversity. It locates this understanding within an emergent theory of liberation. Integral to this theory is the notion that human beings have both the proclivity and capacity for liberation. Liberation reflects human relations devoid of coercion, domination, subordination, and manipulation. Such relations are nonhierarchical. Diversity is an artifact of liberation. I define diversity relationally; diversity is a relation between human beings. It reflects a relation to others that is characterized by empathy, compassion, openness, and trust. It is a relation that catalyzes evolution and transformation. *Diversity reflects relations that allow for the communion of differences.* This definition of diversity assumes that human beings are fundamentally relational beings with the striving and potentiality for communion. I argue that to look at diversity this way expands our understanding of the potential of human beings.

What most distinguishes this emergent theory of liberation from that of others is the foregrounding of the position that human beings have an existential and spiritual proclivity and capacity for liberation. Existential strivings represent any quality that is uniquely human. In other words, human beings possess a set of strivings that are uniquely human and point to us having a special relation to the world. Most discussions of liberation, by focusing exclusively on the political, undercut consideration of liberation as an existential and spiritual striving. I posit that this existential and spiritual deficiency morally bankrupts most discussions of liberation and severely limits our understanding of liberation. Implicitly, such discussions suggest no connection between liberation and being, reinforcing the belief that human beings have no existential and spiritual need for liberation. We find a fixation with structures and institutions rather than with human beings. This secular orientation undermines the possibility of new and different understandings of liberation. The result is that popular understandings of liberation pose no real threat to the status quo.

Nothing found in the following pages of this book represents a disavowal of politics. We are political beings, for politics is the negotiation of representation or the articulation of being. All acts of negotiation are about representation. Identity is the corollary of representation and politics is the negotiation of identity. I focus on the discursive and material practices that affirm our existential and spiritual strivings. Discursive practices refer to the ideas, values, beliefs, truths, assumptions, hopes, and fears that fashion our ways of being. Only those practices that complement our existential and spiritual strivings are ethical and moral. In assuming that a moral benchmark exists, I reject moral relativism. In my view, without assuming that human beings are moral, existential, and spiritual beings, what constitutes the political will always be ethically and morally adrift. The result will be exactly what now exists; that is, moral relativism, fatalism, and nihilism.

I posit no causal relation between discursive and material practices that I consider liberatory and the realization of liberation. This kind of determinism distorts what being human means by suggesting that human beings lack the ability to act deliberately upon the world. Instead, I view human beings as complex beings who are simultaneously dealing with matters of volition, physiological and biological needs, existential and spiritual strivings, mental and physical states, and an array of discursive and material practices. I contend that such a complex definition of being enriches our understanding of liberation. Such a definition reveals, among other things, how human beings aid and abet the construction of structures to limit the exercising of volition so as to avoid responsibility for actions based on fear. It offers a superior approach for understanding the nature and origin of structures. Most discussions of liberation suggest that structures that thwart liberation can simply be replaced with other structures. Such an approach assumes that liberation merely rests with the evolution of new structures. In underestimating how much the possibility of liberation demands of us, this approach fosters helplessness, cynicism, despair, and, ultimately, hopelessness. Such outcomes eventually make for desperation, which often takes the form of violent conflict. Although new structures sometimes appear after the conflict has subsided, the promise of liberation never materializes, which makes for the return of helplessness, hopelessness, and so forth. However, on the other hand, a complex definition of being suggests that the possibility of liberation demands a lot from all of us.

Our proclivity and capacity to bring meaning to bear on the world is an existential and spiritual striving. To bring meaning to bear on the world represents an act of creation. The underlying assumption is that human beings have the ability to help with the completion of the world and, conversely, that the world has been left unfinished. To look at meaning creation as an existential and spiritual striving represents an emergent definition of communication. Popular definitions of communication assume no distinction between animals and human beings. What sustains such popular views of communication are the beliefs that human beings are aexistential, aspiritual, and amoral. It is commonly believed that communication is an artifact of necessity. Supposedly, communication evolved out of the need for coordination so as to establish relations with others—either for protection or acquisition of resources, alliances, and mates—that are necessary for our survival. It is also commonly believed that communication evolved out of the need for manipulation so as to increase our chances of survival. Communication is a tool, an artifact of being, something secular. Thus, no sacred relation supposedly exists between communication and being.

The popular view of communication also assumes that communication moves linearly through and along a medium via codes and symbols that contain our thoughts. Its manipulation has no effect on the human condition. The transmission metaphor emerges. It is believed that good communication requires symbols and codes that are ahistorical and acontextual (acultural) so as to afford coordination through transmission of cognitive parcels. Clarity and fidelity are hallmarks of *good* communication. In short, *good* communication supposedly moves effortlessly and smoothly between human beings. The corollary is that language must be beyond subjectivity and possess a consistency that must be beyond any kind of corruption. A civilized and evolved language—supposedly reflecting civilized and evolved peoples—is supposedly one that is standardized, meaning that civilized and evolved peoples seek to sustain a standardized language. Without standardization, then, the *good society* is supposedly undermined. The goal is for language to correspond to an objective reality that is presumably constant and predetermined. Progress results from knowing the ways of this objective reality so that claims can be *objectively proven* and truths made universally generalizable and transferable. Consequently, without a standardized language, human progress is undermined.

Popular understandings of both communication and language reflect a common worldview. Both draw upon a common set of beliefs, assumptions, and truths of the world. Both also reflect and engender a certain understanding of what being human means and our relation to each other and the world. To contend that human beings have an existential and spiritual striving to bring meaning to bear on the world is to point to a different worldview and a different understanding of communication and language. Instead of clarity and fidelity, *good* communication is assessed by degrees of empathy, flexibility, and transparency. Focus is on maintaining vibrant and transparent meaning creation processes. A *sacred* relation is assumed between communication and being as both our humanity and our world are constituted through communication. In this way, I reject the commonly held belief that languages can be corrupted and that certain languages are highly complex and others less. I reject the other assumptions that undergird such reasoning. In brief, I reject our fixation with symbols and codes. I also reject the commonly held belief that language is an artifact of necessity. I contend that our understanding of language needs to be reconstituted to reflect emergent truths of the world. Rather than fixed and predetermined, the world ebbs and flows. Accordingly, our languages must also have the capacity to ebb and flow. This demands a new relation to our languages. I call for a relational understanding of language. I develop the argument that any emergent definition of liberation that is existentially and spiritually based calls forth different understandings of communication and language. I aim to show that such understandings are integral to an emergent understanding of diversity.

Discussions of liberation deal dismally with the question of diversity. We find a resorting to a myriad of specious theoretical schemes. Nothing firm exists. Popular discourses about diversity—assimilation versus toleration—delimit our understanding of diversity through a hegemony of secular assumptions. I argue that when our understanding of diversity is undercut, our understanding of liberation is also undercut. Consequently, I respond critically to contemporary proponents of assimilation and toleration. I contend that both discourses—regardless of the various versions and permutations—lack any kind of firm theoretical ground. The result is that both discourses reflect paradoxes, confusions, theoretical shortcomings, and other theoretical mishaps that undercut any understanding of diversity as a potentially existential and spiritual phenomenon that bespeaks an existential and spiritual world. Further, both discourses give us a distorted understanding of diversity, which is to say that diversity is supposedly purely about *differences*, such as race, ethnicity, sexual orientation, and so forth. Such differences, however, are preconditions of diversity.

I contend that our deep distrust and suspicion of our humanity makes for a deep distrust and suspicion of diversity. This fear and distrust is aptly captured in both dominant discourses about diversity. Although assimilation and toleration are commonly seen as representing conflicting positions and different politics, nothing about the differences is significant. It is really about degrees of distrust of diversity. In brief, proponents of assimilation contend that homogeneity is supposedly vital for unity. However, the homogeneity that assimilation engenders undercuts life by ending diversity that is vital for growth, development, and transformation. On the other hand, toleration discourses rest on the assumption that this is a world of contradictions, paradoxes, and dilemmas. Proponents contend that only ad hoc solutions are possible. This argument, however, is also bereft of any compelling reason as to why diversity is life affirming. Proponents of toleration also give us no compelling existential or spiritual argument for diversity. Moreover, both sets of discourses limit diversity to *differences*—mostly cultural, racial, and gender—that must be managed for the good of all. Diversity is rarely cast as something moral, existential, and spiritual. Further, both sets of discourses reify a deep fear of diversity. Finally, neither assimilation nor toleration poses any threat to the status quo. In fact, both block scrutiny of the status quo by limiting diversity to differences that must be secularly managed for the good of all to avoid chaos and social devolution. This secular orientation to diversity conceals domination by allowing a certain set of beliefs, values, and assumptions to go uninterrogated.

To get beyond what I consider the quagmires of dominant discourses about diversity, a new set of assumptions is required. I posit that a new set of assumptions transforms our understanding of diversity. Diversity affirms our existential and spiritual strivings. It strives when empathy, compassion, trust, and kindness blossom. It represents the blossoming of our existential and spiritual strivings. Diversity is also vital for unity, or unity is an artifact of diversity. It is an artifact of *only* a certain set of discursive and material practices, specifically those that are fundamentally moral. Diversity represents the end of hierarchy. As diversity can only unfold organically, this means that unity also evolves with the end of hierarchy.

The problem is with *otherness* rather than with diversity. I focus on the origins of otherness. I contend that otherness represents the undercutting of what Erich Fromm (1973) refers to as our natural striving for union. This striving resembles what Paulo Freire (1993) refers to as our striving for *human completion*. Our striving for union represents an existential striving to foster deep and complex relations to the world and with others. Its blocking threatens our destruction. Otherness represents separation; it is the reifying of our differences. Otherness is about distrust, suspicion, and fear and it represents the negation of diversity. It is through the overcoming of separation that human beings become fully human. I focus on the discursive and material practices that engender separation and, conversely, those that engender union. Obviously, separation is the status quo. We are afraid of union. We are of a worldview that undercuts the discursive and material practices that are vital to the blossoming of this striving. We also lack the consciousness and temperament necessary to deal with this natural striving.

The overcoming of separation demands the forging of deep and meaningful relations. This is the aspiration of our striving for union. In this way, our striving for union fosters unity rather than the end of diversity, which only blossoms through the forging of deep and meaningful human relations. Race, ethnicity, gender, sexual orientation, and so forth reflect real differences, different ways of perceiving and relating to the world and each other. But such differences by no means make naturally for diversity. I view diversity as the blossoming of union: it reflects human beings who have acquired a deep capacity for affirmation, empathy, compassion, and trust; it is organically nonhierarchical. Differences and diversity are entwined. The real task is to construct relations that allow us to move beyond our differences to new differences so as to avoid entrapping each other to our race, sexuality, gender, ethnicity, and so on. Diversity is about forging relations that continuously increase and expand our capacity to look at the world differently.

The primary objective of this project is to present an emergent understanding of diversity. I present and critique contemporary understandings of diversity found in dominant discourses of diversity and multiculturalism within the United States. I address understandings that span the theoretical and political spectrum. We will find that all sides of the political and theoretical spectrum look at diversity as differences. I aim to show how such contemporary understandings of diversity make for a narrow and morally deficient view of diversity. I focus on the worldview origins of contemporary understandings of diversity. Worldviews fashion our relation to each and the world. I contend that our problems with diversity can be traced to our worldview. Conversely, any emergent understanding of diversity is obligated to also present an emergent worldview. I unpack this emergent worldview.

What strangles dominant discourses of diversity is the lack of interrogation of fundamental assumptions of the world that subtly yet powerfully shape our understanding of the world. This lack of interrogation serves to narrow understandings of diversity, thereby neutralizing any real threat to the status quo. Besides giving us a shallow and narrow understanding of diversity, diversity as differences legitimizes a politics and ethics of separation. The status quo thrives on this politics and ethics. I address the mechanics of this legitimation. I aim to show that any understanding of diversity limited to differences poses no real threat to the status quo. As Audre Lorde (1984) observed, "The master's tools will never dismantle the master's house." We need new tools. We need an understanding of diversity that moves beyond differences. This is the mission of this project. I offer an emergent definition that provides us the opportunity for a politics and ethics premised on union rather than separation. I contend that only such an ethics and politics affirms life. The distinguishing features of this politics and ethics is the end of hierarchy and domination. In this regard, this emergent understanding of diversity poses a direct threat to the status quo. This is also why this emergent understanding of diversity is drawn from an emergent understanding of liberation.

Casting diversity in relation to the affirmation of life points to how I enter this project. I am concerned with what a politics and ethics of separation does to our humanity. I view the effects of separation as real and debilitating. I contend that separation weakens our humanness, our ability to construct and sustain nonhierarchical relations. It stifles what most makes us human, namely our proclivity and capacity to develop deep and complex relations with the world and each other through meaning creation. I am beyond concerns of representation. In my view, the stakes are higher and bear directly on the condition of the world. It is a matter fundamentally of realizing our full potential as existential and spiritual and moral beings.

This project unfolds around a case study, or what I prefer to view as a kind of background narrative. Its purpose is to give us the opportunity to get beyond the abstraction of theory. The case study is the controversy that arose in reaction to a resolution by the Oakland School Board in December 1996. I focus predominantly on the reaction rather than the resolution. This controversy aptly captures the ethics and politics of separation. It nakedly, and in a vulgar manner, reveals the fundamental assumptions that fashion our view of the world and, as a result, make for our narrow understanding of diversity. What also makes the controversy especially compelling is the near unanimous disgust and horror against the resolution. Rarely does a controversy make for near unanimous protest. Equally striking was the visceral nature of the reaction. No explanation from either scholars or the school board ameliorated the reaction. The school board was forever condemned. Moreover, the controversy reveals how a narrow understanding of diversity pervades all sides of the theoretical and political spectrum.

Both traditional proponents and opponents of diversity condemned the resolution for the exact same reasons. Rarely does a subject make for such common ground between both groups. The controversy also reveals the narrowness of dominant discourses of diversity occurring within the United States and how this narrowness serves the status quo. I discuss why both traditional proponents and opponents of diversity responded identically. Also, the controversy reveals how a politics and ethics of separation emasculates our potential for union. It was no accident that the reaction was devoid of empathy and compassion, because a politics of separation legitimizes and engenders this kind of aggression. I use the Oakland controversy to show also how this kind of reaction reduces our humanness: A politics and ethics of separation thwarts our civility; it blocks our questing for communion through community. No doubt the politics and ethics can be seen in other situations, such as debates over prison and education reform. However, the Oakland controversy is uniquely rich for the reasons just stated.

I also use a writing style that hopefully makes the book widely accessible. I make no assumptions regarding what readers know about the matters I address. I have left no scholarly term undefined and have sought to make my arguments succinct and clear. I want my arguments to be engaged by all kinds of audiences. Also, I have found that a writing style that strenuously stresses clarity improves rigor by committing the writer to account for the origins of assumptions that sustain arguments and are too often left unexamined. Clarity forces us to address constantly the question of why. In my own writing and teaching experiences, I have found that this exercise exposes many gaps in my reasoning that bear directly on the credibility of my arguments and how I present an argument. Finally, the writing style reflects my belief that this book offers pathways that have the potential to help us heal the world and each other. It is by no means a scholarly contemplation on the condition of the world. I come to this project from a racial, cultural, social, and political standpoint that obligates my labor to projects that help end practices that sustain both human suffering and misery. As regards the condition of the world, I concur with the view that neutrality is a dangerous myth.

1

The Narrative

The resolution was heard around the world. On December 18, 1996, Oakland Unified School District of California passed a resolution granting legitimacy to something commonly referred to as *Black English* or *Ebonics* (Appendix A). The public reaction to this resolution was overwhelmingly negative and visceral. The reaction evolved quickly into an uproar as persons from all races, social classes, educational backgrounds, and political stripes saw the decision as a threat to the *good society*. There was almost unanimous protest against the ruling. The school board was accused of being ignorant, irresponsible, and incompetent. Although the school board released a clarifying statement (Appendix B) to quell the uproar, especially within the black community, the attacks continued unrelentingly. The reaction was akin to a public flogging, as the following published comments suggest:

> Elevating black English to the status of a language is not the way to raise standards of achievement in our schools and for our students. It has been determined by the United States Department of Education and the Clinton administration that the use of federal bilingual education funds for what has been called black English or ebonics is not permitted.
> Education Secretary Richard Riley

Normally when the academic failure of black children is taken into this zone, it quickly ignites obligation in government agencies, foundations, universities, school districts, and the like. Money flows, jobs materialize, careers advance, and so on. When ebonics finally made the national news, several fully funded ebonics programs were already up and running in California and elsewhere. Had ebonics not become a laughing-stock, it might have thrived as a moderately profitable idea. Indeed, there will still likely be profit taking in the form of MLA (Modern Language Association) papers on the hermeneutics of ebonics, linguistic investigations into the African roots of the language, grants given to examine it as a teaching device, conferences, and more. Even its rough ride in the media will likely not banish ebonics entirely from the zone of opportunism.

  Shelby Steele, Hoover Institute, Stanford University

I understand the attempt to reach out to these children, but this is an unacceptable surrender, borderlining on disgrace. It's teaching down to our children and it must never happen. I appeal to that board to please reverse that decision because they're becoming really, unfortunately, the laughingstock of the nation.

  Rev. Jesse Jackson

It is saying in the most racist way that black kids are stupid and they can't learn English so let's not bother with that. These kids deserve a little better than the latest social engineering scheme.

  Jim Boulet, English First

We are appalled. They are creating a subculture that will never learn any kind of responsibility to society.

  Margo Koller, Tucson, Arizona

I think it's tragic.

  Ward Connerly, Regent, University of California

Ebonics is not a foreign or distinct language. It should neither be taught in the classroom, nor accommodated there.

  Sen. Ray Haynes, Riverside

I be thinking that [Ebonics] be real ignorant.

  Spike Lee

Ignoromics.

  Bill Cosby

Quite frankly, the Oakland strategy seems to be pedagogy run amok. . . . We in this country need to catch ourselves. . . . Neither our nation, nor our nation of children, has the time for this.
  A.J. Verdelle, Bunting Institute, Harvard University

If Oakland's School Board accomplished nothing else, it gave people . . . something to laugh at over the holidays.
  Ellis Cose, *Newsweek*

I think the (Ebonics) program is stupid. It underestimates people and says they can't learn English. It excludes one group from everyone else.
  Tamika Hurd, Mountain View-Los Altos Union High School District

I think this is academic hogwash, and it's a scam and a fraud.
  Robert Woodson, Chad School Foundation

[T]he notion of Ebonics [is] patronizing, divisive and destructive to the very people it is meant to assist. . . . It doesn't preserve pride. It preserves isolation and segregation.
  Erica Meyer Rauzin, Jewish Press

Those probably best qualified to comment on the pedagogical merit of the ruling, specifically linguists, somehow never had equal access to the popular media forums that opponents to the ruling had. So only few heard that The Linguistic Society of America (1997), the representing body for linguists, unanimously endorsed the resolution with a statement that concluded:

In fact, all human linguistic systems—spoken, signed, and written— are fundamentally regular. The systematic and expressive nature of the grammar and pronunciation patterns of the African American vernacular has been established by numerous scientific studies over the past thirty years. . . . [T]he Oakland School Board's decision to recognize the vernacular of African American students in teaching them Standard English is linguistically and pedagogically sound. (p. 1)

It seems then that the school board was merely heeding the words of James Baldwin. In a 1979 *New York Times* essay, Baldwin (1997) observed:

It is not the black child's language that is in question, it is not his language that is despised: It is his experience. A child cannot be taught by anyone who despises him, and a child cannot be taught by anyone whose demand, essentially, is that the child repudiate his experience, and all that gives him sustenance, and enter a limbo in which he will no longer be black, and in which he knows that he can never become white. Black people have lost too many black children that way. (p. 6)

The reaction raises matters that are fundamentally moral, existential, and spiritual in origin. The controversy strikingly reveals the fundamental assumptions, values, beliefs, and truths that undergird our understanding of the *good society*. No doubt endless dissertations, theses, research papers, and other scholarly papers will be written about the controversy, along with many literary, political, and cultural analyses. I, however, use the controversy, albeit fortuitously, merely as an opportunity to help expound an emergent theory of diversity that is drawn from an emergent theory of liberation. It is used purely for backdrop. Any controversy that was comparably fecund and popular would have sufficed.

The definition of liberation I adopt contests commonly held assumptions, beliefs, truths, and values. Liberation reflects human relations devoid of domination, subordination, and manipulation, that is, hierarchy. Hierarchy is an arrangement based on the suppression of the open expression of conflict and differences rather than biological differences as is commonly assumed by paleontologists, sociobiologists, psychobiologists, and others. As Murray Bookchin (1995) observes, "A hierarchy is based on domination by institutionalized strata, such as gerontocracies, patriarchies, warrior modalities, shamanistic guilds, priestly corporations, and the like over subjugated strata who are visibly underprivileged on an ongoing basis" (p. 49).

To view liberation as any relation devoid of domination also contests the popular definition of liberation as autonomy. In *On Matters of Liberation* (2000) I argued that liberation as autonomy represents a shallow understanding of liberation. Autonomy is a myth. We are fundamentally relational beings. The potential of our humanity is entwined with the humanity of others. I argued that this relation has an existential and spiritual origin. As much as this relation now seems to limit us, the reality is that within this relation also resides the potential to afford the highest level of being. The problem is with hierarchy rather than the lack of autonomy. Liberation as autonomy assumes that human beings are aexistential and aspiritual and amoral beings. It trades in a cheap currency of what being human means. Its increasing popularity can be attributed to the fact that it releases us of any responsibility and commitment to the well-being of others. Liberation as autonomy legitimizes selfishness, greed, competition, distrust, and hierarchy, which explains why the institutions of the elites of wealth and power are increasingly peddling this view of liberation.

Liberation as autonomy also leaves uninterrogated the deep ideological structures that surreptitiously constrain our being. It legitimizes rather than delegitimizes the status quo. In *On Matters of Liberation*, besides critiquing hierarchy as a *truth* of the world, I sought to account for the evolution of this truth, the ideology that sustains this truth, and show how this truth is purely a social construction, an artifact of our own worldview. I argued, for example, that this truth is alien to the worldviews of many native peoples throughout the world. Accordingly, I argued for an emergent worldview which I then set about sketching with broad strokes. In this second book, this sketching continues.

I call for an existential and spiritual conception of our humanity. I focus on the discursive and material practices that complement such a conception. The result is a new kind of human relations and a different relation to the world. In this manuscript, however, I focus exclusively on the features of an emergent human relations. I contend that our common conception of our humanity reflects what I refer to as a secular hegemony. According to Stanley Deetz (1995), "*Hegemony* is . . . a complex web of conceptual and material arrangements producing the very fabric of everyday life, the perceptions of events, the presence of common-sense knowledge, and conventional wisdom" (p. 165, italics in original). Simply put, hegemony is about accepting subordination as norm. I refer to a secular hegemony as one that engenders the belief that human beings are aexistential and aspiritual beings. The reaction to the school board ruling compellingly reveals the nature of this secular hegemony. In my view, this is what makes the controversy especially compelling.

Explicit within the reaction to the school board is the belief that human beings possess a proclivity for chaos and social devolution. The corollary is that coercion and hierarchy are vital for progress and social evolution. Opponents of the ruling assumed that Ebonics is an artifact of our supposed proclivity for *chaos* and *social devolution*. It reflects backwardness. It also supposedly harms cognitive development. Many opponents made such a claim. Ebonics is seen as lacking the sophistication to afford progress and social evolution. Its fluidity, flexibility, and spontaneity are seen as threats to the development of complex rational thought. It is supposedly the *language* of the uneducated, the uncultured, and the unsophisticated. The implication is that the school board was legitimizing racist myths by formally tying blacks to a language that is assumed to be backward. It is no doubt for this reason that the reaction of the black community was the most visceral and critical. The reaction of the black community captures the anxiety of blacks about being seen as less equal to whites. This anxiety is a legacy of over 350 years of institutional racism and discrimination.

The school board was supposedly pandering to our proclivity for chaos and devolution. The reaction reflects the belief that human beings are devoid of any natural moral striving. Left to our own volition and devices, the world will supposedly descend towards chaos and destruction, and human beings toward animality and bestiality. Consequently, hierarchy is necessary for the evolution of the good society, as human beings have to be forcefully controlled and ordered. The lack of any natural moral capacity means that human beings have to be secularly equipped with moral codes. The elites of wealth and power are increasingly contending that the competition of market forces represents the best way to do this. Integral to this ordering and controlling is the managing of our differences, which contributes to our deep distrust of them. The corollary is that homogeneity is vital to progress and social evolution. The point is that the reaction to the Oakland resolution shows us exercising a politics and ethics that assumes that human beings are devoid of any existential, spiritual and moral capacity to act nonhierarchically.

The Oakland controversy presents a compelling opportunity to discuss all that is fundamentally wrong with this secular hegemony and how our own worldview undercuts our existential and spiritual strivings. This is how the controversy functions as a beachhead. Our attention turns now to explicating the origins of our deep distrust and suspicion of differences. Such origins can be found in what Erich Fromm (1956) refers to as *human separation*. Human separation reflects human relations that disconnect us from each other through fear, distrust, suspicion, and apathy. The hallmark of such relations is hierarchy. I aim to show how separation makes us less human and, therefore, less civil. Separation explains the visceral hostility that characterized the reaction to the resolution. I also focus on how separation makes for a politics and ethics of separation by undermining the evolution of deep and meaningful relations. I discuss the perilous effects of this politics and ethics on our humanity. Ultimately, I aim to show how the reaction poignantly reflects the hegemony of this politics and ethics of separation.

2

The Nature
of Civility

Ebonics . . . is . . . just ungrammatical English spoken by people who
haven't been taught properly. The cure for that is not to rename it or
look for ways to boost the speakers' self-esteem but to teach them
the right way.
    Editorial, *Chicago Tribune*

The idea [of critics] is that dialect speakers could speak better if they
tried, if they were more careful, if they would only pay more attention to what they're saying. The best way to correct this, of course, is
to scold them.
    Charles Fillmore, Professor of Linguistics, University of
    California, Berkeley

In my opinion, however, this is settling for mediocrity. For this
brand of pernicious nonsense [separatist poison] to be extended to
seven-year-olds should be chilling to all thinking people.
    John McWhorter, Professor of Linguistics and African American
    Studies, University of California, Berkeley

R egardless of whether the resolution was wrong or dumb, why did the Oakland school board have to be ridiculed, abused, threatened, and coerced? What accounts for the resorting to bombast, aggression, and coercion by opponents? What about the ruling was so threatening to stir such visceral hostility? The reaction to the resolution shows no qualitative distinction from the reaction other groups have historically faced for simply being cast as Other. It all raises the following questions: Why is hostility the dominant reaction to any perceived threat to stability and homogeneity? What gives this kind of reaction legitimacy? What are the mechanisms of legitimation? Why the lack of empathy and compassion? In fact, why Other?

In what follows I contend that our dominant consciousness of the world undermines our capacity for civility by engendering and reifying human separation. It is this separation that makes for the origin of otherness. To be cast as Other is ultimately to be cast as a threat to social evolution and progress. The origins of human separation can be traced to our deep distrust and suspicion of our humanity. We believe that human beings have a natural proclivity for chaos and social devolution. Consequently, coercion is seen as vital to the evolution of the good society. It supposedly fosters civility. Conversely, the lack of civility supposedly reflects a lack of coercion. Intimidation, domination, hostility, and aggression are all manifestations of coercion. In brief, the reaction to the school board was, unfortunately, no anomaly.

I develop the thesis that separation engenders disunity rather than unity, aggression rather than compassion, nihilism rather than optimism, oppression rather than liberation. What is required is the evolution of a new worldview and a new consciousness, as our ways of relating to each other are entwined with our relation to the world. Accordingly, who constitutes the Other, and what justifications are used to determine the Other, are merely arbitrary social constructions. We thus have no need to concern ourselves with the credibility of the endless justifications used to sustain various distinctions that make for Otherness. This approach to sexism, racism, heterosexism, tribalism, and so forth is simply misplaced. Any of us can always qualify as Other based on any number of arbitrary justifications.

THE CONSTRUCTION OF OTHERNESS

Negative reactions against Ebonics and the Oakland School Board . . . reflect racist assumptions about the language and educational needs of Black working-class and un-working-class people. . . . Assault on the language of African America is a way of reinscribing the subordination and powerlessness of Black working-class people in this country.

Geneva Smitherman, University Distinguished Professor of English, Michigan State University

We are not teaching pig Latin. We are not teaching Ebonics. We are not teaching anything except standard English. But what we do want is our youngsters to come to school and not feel that they are inferior because they do not speak standard English. We will not devalue the child because they do not come to us with standard English.

Lucella Harrison, President, Oakland School Board

Otherness represents the reification of human separation. This view assumes that human beings have a natural, that is, existential and spiritual, striving for union and fusion. In The Art of Loving, Erich Fromm (1956) writes, "This desire for interpersonal fusion is the most powerful striving in man. It is the most fundamental passion, it is the force which keeps the human race together, the clan, the family, society. The failure to achieve it means insanity or destruction—self-destruction of others" (p. 17). We need look no further than the research on touching to affirm this striving for fusion and the negative consequences that occur when this striving is undermined. Quantity and quality of touching significantly affects cognitive, emotional, and physical development (Field, 1998). Case in point: Cultures with higher degrees of touching tend to have less levels of criminality and animality (Colt, 1997). We are, however, deeply embedded within a worldview that fosters human separation.

Our discursive and material practices reveal a condition of separation. We show a discomfort with any kind of deep and profound expression of affection and affirmation. We are of the conviction that gender, race, ethnicity, and sexual orientation are real differences that justify discrimination and hierarchy. We view liberation individually rather than communally or even relationally. We fear that the forging of deep and meaningful relations demands sacrifices and compromises. We have, as a result, reduced relationships to networks, peoples to markets, neighborhoods to enclaves, and so on. The point is that our consciousness of the world reeks with anxiety about union. Fromm contends that separation undercuts our ability to act deliberately upon the world by thwarting our natural striving to affirm life. Separation fosters anxiety and helplessness. Our ability to act deliberately upon the world, according to Fromm, is entwined with being fully human. Through union human beings become fully human. Being fully human is defined as our capacity to construct and sustain nonhierarchical relations. This definition assumes that the striving for such relations resides within human beings. In Anatomy of Human Destructiveness, a book that numerous critics view as a masterful study of the human condition, Fromm (1973) develops the argument that hierarchy thwarts human development: "The history of mankind is, indeed, a history of the fight for freedom. . . . Freedom is the condition for the full growth of a person, for his mental health and his well-being; its absence cripples man and is unhealthy" (p. 225).

Fromm (1973) proceeds to posit that liberation is a vital biological human need that human beings strive to fulfill:

> As a condition for the unstunted development of the human organism, freedom is a vital biological interest of man, and threats to his freedom arouse defensive aggression as do all other threats to human interests. Is it surprising then all aggression and violence continue to be generated in a world in which the majority are deprived of freedom, especially the people in the so-called underdeveloped countries? Those in power—i.e., the whites—would perhaps be less surprised and indignant if they were not accustomed to considering the yellows, the browns and the blacks as nonpersons and, hence, not expected to react humanly. (p. 226)

Fromm cautions that our attempts to fulfill this need for liberation can also make for dysfunctional practices that thwart freedom. As with any other vital human need, this need for freedom also has to be properly nurtured:

> The fact that genuine revolutionary aggression, like all aggression generated by the impulse to defend one's life, freedom or dignity, is biologically rational and part of normal human functioning must not deceive one into forgetting that destruction of life remains destruction, even when it is biologically justified; it is a matter of one's religious, moral, or political principles whether one believes that it is humanly justified or not. But whatever one's principles in this respect are, it is important to be aware how easily purely defensive aggression is blended with (nondefensive) destructiveness and with the sadistic wish to reverse the situation by controlling others instead of being controlled. If and when this happens, revolutionary aggression is vitiated and tends to renew the conditions it was seeking to abolish. (p. 226)

Separation undermines diversity. The anxiety that springs from separation can be seen in our fear to be different and our encumbering of others to be different. Separation heightens our deep distrust and anxiety of differences. In this way, the suppression of diversity begins with the suppression of our humanity. We project our fears upon others, afraid that the expression of any kind of diversity will expose our own fears. We also suppress diversity by thwarting the open expression of conflict. We fear that conflict threatens stability and homogeneity. Conflict supposedly represents chaos. The corollary is that diversity represents chaos. We also suppress diversity by thwarting our striving for union. We do so by starving our relations of affirmation, empathy, compassion, respect, and trust. Diversity is undermined through the undercutting of our striving for union. What emerges is a society that adheres to a worldview that reinforces a consciousness of separation and engenders our subordination to our creations. The result is hierarchy.

Hierarchy is the antithesis of union. It is the hallmark of separation. In On Matters of Liberation, I argued that hierarchy is born of our deep distrust and suspicion of our humanity. It is an artifact of fear. Hierarchy blocks the evolution of our existential strivings by thwarting the evolution of deep and meaningful human relations. The natural outcomes of such relations are equality, diversity, and cooperation. Realizing such relations demands ways of being laden with empathy, compassion, transparency, and affirmation. Hierarchy, however, blocks such ways of being. It cultivates deception, the reason being that transparency blocks manipulation. Without deception, hierarchy is undermined. Accordingly, hierarchy reflects and reinforces our fear and discomfort with union and it undercuts our striving for union. It represents the destruction of ourselves and each other. Hierarchy also undercuts diversity by fostering conformity and homogeneity. It does so by suppressing the open expression of conflict. Indeed, history compellingly reveals that peoples who have systematically persecuted other groups based on arbitrary distinctions tend to have a deep hierarchical ethos and are characterized by complex and rigid hierarchical relations and structures.

Inequality is an artifact of hierarchy. Without hierarchy, the elites of wealth and power have no means of organizing the many to gain selfishly. Hierarchy affords the manipulation, subordination, and domination of the many so that a few can gain selfishly. The elites of wealth and power need hierarchy so as to commit the labor of others to tasks and processes that are physically exhausting, cognitively numbing, and spiritually paralyzing. The primary task of elites is increasingly to sustain unobtrusively the control of labor (Barker, 1993; Deetz, 1995; Mumby, 1988; Stohl & Sotirin, 1989; Tompkins & Cheney, 1983). The means of doing so is now elaborately complex and also now transcends the physical spaces of the organization. Zavarzadeh and Morton (1994) discuss how the primary mission of our educational system is "to develop the affective makeup of the labor force, to produce in the labor force the kind of (ideological) consciousness that situates the subject of labor in a manner necessary for the reproduction and maintenance of existing social relations" (p. 142, italics in original). In sum, capital is increasingly outflanking labor. A lot of this outflanking is occurring discursively, through the shaping of beliefs, assumptions, hopes, fears, and ways of being that favor capital. In Frameworks of Power, Stewart Clegg (1989) contends that the outflanking is a result of a lack of knowledgeable resources, making for a lack of options:

> Frequently those who are relatively powerless remain so because they are ignorant of the ways of power: ignorant, that is, of matters of strategy, such as assessing the resources of the antagonist, of routine procedures, rules, agenda setting, access, of informal conduits as well as formal protocols, of the style and substance of power. It is not that they do not know the rules of the game; they might not recognize the game, let alone know the rules. (p. 221)

It is always the few who profit the most from hierarchy. The few, however, need to mask this truth. Deception is vital. The many must be convinced that all persons gain equally from hierarchy. A superior way of accomplishing this myth is by engendering and reifying the belief that hierarchy is vital to afford the evolution of the good society. Capital thrives on our belief that hierarchy blocks the onset of chaos and social devolution. It is supposedly an artifact of progress and a vital calculus for human evolution. The result is domination and exploitation emerging as superior options to annihilation and destruction. But now consideration of evils and lesser evils has disappeared completely from the equation. It is now capital/labor relations or destruction. Such is the new found power of capital. In addition to engendering a belief about the need for hierarchy, capital must also engender a temperament among labor that sustains hierarchy. This kind of temperament entails accepting subordination, manipulation, and domination as the norm and even good. This is hegemony. Labor must also be predisposed to conforming, even willing to end any differences that threaten the status quo. According to Fromm (1956), "It [capital] needs men who feel free and independent, not subject to any authority or principle or conscience—yet willing to be commanded, to do what is expected of them, to fit into the social machine without friction; who can be guided without force, led without leaders, prompted without aim—except the one to make good, to be on the move, to function, to go ahead" (p. 77). The rise of capital—as seen by the tremendous transfer of wealth from the bottom to the top—reflects the deepening subordination of labor. It all shows capital increasingly possessing superior means, techniques, and mechanisms to engender and sustain the obedient subordination of labor. Yet, when labor is reduced to a commodity, human beings are atomized (Deetz, 1995).

But the rise of capital is by no means purely due to the conniving doings of the few inflicted upon a hapless many. Unfortunately, separation, or our own troubles with overcoming separation, makes us amenable to the beliefs and temperament of capital and other elites. Our distrust of union, coupled with the lack of the necessary consciousness and social skills vital for the making of union, makes many of the elements vital for the evolution of capital/labor relations an easy sell. No doubt much of the foundation has been provided by organized religions, which have long shaped our consciousness with notions of hierarchy, coercion, domination, and so forth. We have long known the ways of separation, making for what now seems as a natural aversion to union. Capital merely thrives on this situation. The reality is that our aversion to union transcends and precedes capital/labor relations. In this way, capital/labor relations are merely another artifact of separation, the end of which promises no end to the making of Otherness. Consequently, nothing is gained from demonizing capital and other elites; doing so merely serves to further reify the ethos of separation. Capital is also being dehumanized by separation. In the end, all of us suffer equally from separation.

The focus has to be on realizing union rather than ending hierarchy. This orientation affirms our capacity to transcend everything that engenders diversity. Union affirms diversity. Our striving for union reveals something profound about being human and about our relation to the world and each other. Fromm contends that love reflects the highest level of affirmation. Love also represents the fullest expression of being fully human. About the existential relation between love and moral development, Fromm (1956) writes:

> It is hardly necessary to stress the fact that the ability to love as as an of giving depends on the character development of the person. It assumes the attainment of a predominantly productive orientation; in this orientation the person has overcome dependency, narcissistic omnipotence, the wish to exploit others, or to hoard, and has acquired faith in his own human powers, courage to rely on his powers in the attainment of his goals. To the degree that these qualities are lacking, he is afraid of giving himself—hence of loving. (p. 24)

Fromm posits that this striving for love represents the overcoming of human separation. Our capacity to love correlates with the overcoming of human separation. Fromm believes that the primary objective of life must be loving—undercutting those discursive and material practices that engender and reify our differences. Our striving for union represents an ethics. It reveals an existential and moral obligation to others, foremost of which is our need to help each other move beyond separation. This ethics is consistent with the view that human beings have a natural striving for transparency or openness. In brief, Sydney Jourard (1971), Carl Rogers (1980), and others contend that human beings have a natural striving for transparency, and that human and collective development is catalyzed by transparency. As with our striving for union, what aids the blossoming of transparency are human relations that reflect affirmation, empathy, compassion, and trust.

The notion of union and separation gives us a solid framework to expand our understanding of diversity. It allows us to get beyond diversity as merely differences. Diversity as union foregrounds diversity as a relational phenomenon. It reflects a relation to others that is characterized by empathy, compassion, openness, and trust. It is a relation that catalyzes evolution and transformation. Diversity reflects relations that allow for the communion of differences. This definition accents the uniquely complex relational quality that defines human beings. Diversity as union also points to the universals that undergird our humanity without ending the notion of differences. It also points to our common potentiality. We all have, regardless of our differences, the potential to foster union. In this regard, diversity as union presents us with the opportunity to get beyond the politics and ethics of separation. We will find, as our discussion continues, that a politics and ethics of union delegitimizes the status quo. Diversity is entwined with the end of hierarchy; it is an artifact of liberation.

HOMOGENEITY AND OTHERNESS

In an important sense, the Oakland resolution was controversial because it surfaced foundational beliefs about language and language diversity and exposed an alternative, nonmainstream set of beliefs about language and language variation. The questions and comments about Ebonics provided a forum for exposing alternative ways of viewing language and language diversity. Such views, which are derived from the same core of beliefs that govern religion, morality, and ethics, were assumed to be inflexible and unassailable.

Walt Wolfram, William C. Friday Professor, North Carolina State University

A bedrock belief that undergirds our understanding of the good society is that homogeneity is a precondition of unity. This belief assumes that our differences threaten to social chaos and human devolution. At the deepest level this belief assumes that human beings have a proclivity for social chaos and devolution. It is this proclivity that supposedly makes for the evolution of differences. Accordingly, homogeneity and unity have to be coercively nurtured by us. Eventually, a moral obligation emerges to end and delimit differences so as to afford the good society. That is, the engendering of homogeneity through coercion is legitimized.

Thus, deeply embedded in our understanding of the good society is a deep distrust and suspicion of diversity. Tying homogeneity with unity also assumes that the world lacks symmetry and beauty. We must supposedly look to ourselves for answers and solutions to deal with what is supposedly an unruly and harsh world. No existential or spiritual relation is assumed between us and the world; we have been left to our own devices. Even traditional proponents of diversity admit that toleration represents a tenuous framework.

Our emergent diversity ethos evolved from our ambition to end discrimination and prosecution of the Other. It supposedly bespeaks progress, a new-found level of civility, a mark of the goodness of our democracy. We claim proudly that what makes our levels of civility superior is our ambition to protect the minority from the majority. This is supposedly the hallmark of our democracy. Yet our deep belief that diversity forebodes social chaos and human devolution undercuts any means to accept the Other as either equal or good. The Other always represents a threat to the good society. On the other hand, the homogenous many will always be privileged and seen as good. Accordingly, whenever the tension between the heterogenous few and the homogenous many heightens, as all tensions must, what emerges is a contest between good and evil. In this way, our understanding of the good society puts our civility under a constant strain. The possibility of common ground is nonexistent. The reactions to the school board ruling show this plainly and compellingly.

The tension between the heterogenous few and the homogenous many makes for a privileging of homogeneity. The homogenous many naturally seeks to end all tensions and conflicts by homogenizing the heterogenous few (Orbe, 1998). We find constant efforts at homogenizing differences so as to sustain the majority status that our democracy privileges. The Other is always vulnerable and at the mercy of the homogeneous many. The onus is on the Other to act in ways that would warrant mercy and kindness from the homogeneous many. Eventually, the homogenous many develop discursive and material practices to justify the need to engender homogeneity against the threat of diversity. It always escalates to my God being superior to your God. In turn, the heterogeneous few must often resort to trying to convert members of the homogeneous group so as to better fend off the constant assaults from the homogeneous majority and often to gain the dominant status of the homogeneous majority. Ultimately, the tension between the groups escalates to the point of both sides seeking the destruction of the other, and the construction of schemes to justify such destruction. In short, this deadly tension engenders disunity and deception rather than unity and transparency. History compellingly shows that even our best efforts to check the perilous nature of this tension often fail. When this occurs the homogeneous many are no longer willing to show any kind of mercy to the heterogenous few. All semblances of decency are abandoned. The result is fascism and virulent kinds of nationalism.

We have long sought to cast fascism as a kind of aberration. Our democracy is supposedly superior. Qualitatively, however, no real differences exist between fascism and our understanding of democracy. With fascism, and various strains of nationalism, to best justify the legitimacy of the homogeneous many, the Other is explicitly cast as subhuman. Leaving the heterogeneous few unchecked supposedly poses all kinds of threats to the hegemony of the homogeneous many. It is this justification that fashions moral behavior. Accordingly, to stop all potential threats, total elimination—aptly titled the final solution—of the Other is necessary and morally approved.

The matter eventually evolves to one of purity—purity of race, ethnicity, culture, language, religion. When all pretensions are dropped, the Other simply becomes a threat to the purity of the homogeneous many. Purity represents superiority and evolution. In this way, threats to our purity are also threats to the superiority that our democracy privileges. This kind of reasoning assumes that homogeneity is vital to unity. But when the situation reaches the level of being cast in terms of purity, nothing is sacred. The Other no longer just threatens our superior status, but our survival. It is at this level of the contest that moral sanctioning of death camps and other heinous acts of barbarism are legitimized. The goal is to conquer the world so as to rid the planet of all threats to our purity. Using bombast and threats against groups that are perceived as potential threats to our purity will certainly cause no apprehension in the masses.

The resolution adopted by the Oakland school board was seen as a threat to the hegemony of the homogeneous many. Ebonics is seen as a pollutant. It supposedly threatens the purity of our language, Standard English, and in doing so, threatens social evolution and disunity. The school board thus had to be dealt with accordingly, that is, harshly and oppressively. By posing a threat to the purity of Standard English, the school board was also a de facto threat to the hegemony of the homogeneous many, and the good society. The language—that is, Ebonics—had to be cleansed. Thus, unanticipated by the school board, what was intended to be merely a ruling about pedagogy, emerged as a direct attack on the legitimacy, purity, superiority, and hegemony of the homogeneous many. The school board was testing the bounds of our toleration of diversity. It was testing our civility. The reaction to the resolution shows how tenuous is the mercy on which the heterogeneous few must depend, forever dependent on the kindness of the homogenous many, and constantly trying to avoid the wrath of the dominant group. Although the school board never meant to contest the hegemony of the homogeneous many, because it was seen as misbehaving badly, it deserved no mercy. Also, for refusing to succumb apologetically and quickly to the wishes of the homogeneous many, the school board was further abused, ridiculed, and coerced—qualitatively different from the heinous and evil persecution other minority groups have historically faced under fascist and nationalist regimes. Language cleansing is only qualitatively different from other kinds of cleansing.

INSTITUTIONAL BEINGS

If black children in Oakland, California, are doing poorly in school, we don't simply raise our academic expectations of them and work harder at teaching them; we take the problem into this zone of opportunism that contingency opens between the races, and we say they speak a special black language called ebonics. We then ask for federal money to teach this language to their teachers so they can be more sensitive to the racial self-esteem of these students.
   Shelby Steele, Hoover Institute, Stanford University

This particular issue is just shot through with politics. By and large, linguists are not going to get into arguments about what's a language, what's not a language. Language is not a technical term. It is a political and ideological term.
   Wayne O'Neil, Chairman of the Linguistics and Philosophy
   Department, Massachusetts Institute of Technology

We may argue, as we have, about the Board's choice of definitions and phraseology; and there can be reasonable opinions on both sides as to what schools should do about nonstandard dialects and their speakers. But what is unarguable is this: the persistence of this discussion warns us that the world has changed, that power relations have altered in crucial ways; and however the discourse of race, gender, and power is to be conducted in the future, it will be conducted, and carried on by voices new to the debate.

Robin Lakoff, Professor of Linguistics, University of California, Berkeley

The tension between the homogenous many and the heterogenous few always explodes when the latter directly challenges the legitimacy of the status quo. It is then that all civil pretensions are dropped. The Other is blatantly cast as a threat to social evolution, progress, unity, and the good society, and, as a result, must be dealt with harshly. In Slouching Towards Gomorrah: Modern Liberalism and American Decline, Robert Bork (1996) reveals the wrath that the Other confronts when pretensions are dropped:

> What needs to be said is that no other culture in the history of the world has offered the individual as much freedom, as much opportunity to advance; no other culture has permitted homosexuals, nonwhites, and women to play ever-increasing roles in the economy, in politics, in scholarship, in government. What needs to be said is that American culture is Eurocentric, and it must remain Eurocentric or collapse into meaninglessness. Standards of European and American origin are the only possible standards that can hold our society together and keep us a competent nation. If the legitimacy of Eurocentrism is denied, there is nothing else. There are no standards from any other quarter of the Globe that we can agree upon. . . . Yet a single set of standards is essential to a sense of what authority is legitimate, what ideals must be maintained. The alternative to Eurocentrism, then, is fragmentation and chaos. (p. 311)

Our common understanding of civility and democracy reflects a secular morality. Our democracy perpetuates the notion that human beings are beasts by adhering to amoral, aexistential, and aspiritual assumptions. The corollary to believing that human beings are amoral, aexistential, and aspiritual is that institutions are vital for the making of the good society; they reflect the subordination of human beings to complex and rigid structures. The goal is control. Institutional man fears that without complex and rigid structures human beings will succumb to chaos and passion. Continuity will be undercut. We measure progress by the complexity and rigidity of our structures. Such attributes reflect the ability of structures to control our evil proclivities. Conversely, peoples without complex and rigid structures are commonly seen as backward. Institutions reflect our deep distrust and suspicion of our humanity. The result is that institutional man reeks of distrust, fear, and suspicion. He is devoid of any belief in a human capacity for goodness. He is a staunch proponent of the need for law and order, and an equally staunch proponent of what he sees as objective truths, such as IQ and ethnicity. He also prefers that his relations with others and the world be mediated institutionally.

Institutional man is deathly afraid of diversity. He believes that diversity threatens stability and order and he seeks to delimit and end differences through stridency and rigidity. He also seeks homogeneity through uniformity and conformity. The result is that institutional man is devoid of the ability to exercise deep levels of empathy and compassion, but focuses on forging complex and rigid structures rather than deep and meaningful relations. It is, however, only through the exercising of empathy, compassion, and tenderness, that human beings are humanized. It is the development of such attributes that distinguishes human beings from beasts. Accordingly, the forging of deep and meaningful human relations is vital to becoming human. In this way, institutions undercut the blossoming of our existential and spiritual and moral strivings.

Homogeneity thrives when our relations are mediated institutionally rather than relationally. Institutions limit the intensity of human relations by limiting the open expression of conflict, thereby suppressing the catalyst vital for the evolution of diversity. In blocking the evolution of such conflict, institutions block us from acquiring the temperament and techniques vital to constructively managing such conflict. The result is a deep fear of differences. Institutions block us from dealing with our own anxiety about union by affording an environment that spares us from confronting and overcoming that anxiety. Consequently, rather than engaging the children and people of Oakland in a discussion of the factors that led to the resolution, opponents went directly to the most complex and rigid of institutions—Congress—to suppress the ruling. The school board was seen as threatening the integrity of an institution vital for progress and evolution—in this case, the institution of Standard English. The resolution supposedly posed a threat to our progress.

Yet, as already stated, human beings are fundamentally relational beings. Our "relationalness" is akin to what water is for fishes and the sky for birds. To limit our relationalness is to limit the full expression of our humanity. What defines our relationalness is our proclivity and capacity to develop deep and complex relations to the world and each other through meaning creation, which accounts for human beings having religions, sciences, literatures, and cultures. Institutions limit our relationalness by limiting communication. In so doing, institutions reduce us to beasts by suppressing the strivings that make us human.

This condition is exacerbated by the fact that hierarchy legitimizes and fosters a politics and ethics of separation. It fosters a deep distrust and suspicion of our humanity. This fear is used to justify the limiting of our relationalness. The task that confronts us is to develop ways of being that accent our relationalness. This requires communication practices that enliven our relationalness. Institutions will disappear concomitantly with the evolution of union. Diversity begins and ends locally. Every relationship presents us with the opportunity to transform the world and each other through a politics and ethics of union.

THE NATURE OF DIALOGUE

This African American Vernacular English shares most of its grammar and vocabulary with other dialects of English. But it is distinct in many ways, and it is more different from standard English than any other dialect spoken in continental North America. It is not simply slang, or grammatical mistakes, but a well-formed set of rules of pronunciation and grammar that is capable of conveying complex logic and reasoning.
    William Labov, Professor of Linguistics, University of
    Pennsylvania

The bottom line is this: If you have a child in school, do you want them to grow up learning what used to be called the King's English, for what it was worth, to be able to fit into the society that still generally speaks that? Or, should they be allowed to speak some other language, because that's what they want.
    Sam Donaldson, ABC News

It's not a question of whether they should be allowed to speak what is clearly not a language. The fact is, there was a move on the part of some people in Oakland . . . not just to ring money from the federal government, but to contribute to the continuing ghetto-ization of young African Americans, that we now see afoot in schools where they teach a kind of crackpot Afro-centrism. Aristotle was black, Cleopatra was black; perfect rubbish. Now, it's suppose to make people feel good. Well, it won't make them feel good when they go into the job market and can't talk or think clearly.
    George Will, ABC News

Well, I agree with that conclusion, certainly, but I don't agree that Afro-centrism poses that big a threat to American culture.
    Clarence Page, ABC News

Although Oakland is the focus of attention, the issues we have surfaced are national in their scope. You cannot talk about issues of educational achievement of African American children in urban America without also addressing issues of race, poverty, language, and immigration. Unfortunately, it is clear from the rhetoric surrounding this issue that we have not yet learned how to deal with the real issues of urban education in a respectful, coherent and logical way. . . . Our focus on African American student achievement is all the more compelling because of the fact that if we find ways to help the least successful students, we will benefit all of our students. Every moment lost is a child lost. In the midst of this debate, our community has stood together and proclaimed that the loss of a single child is no longer acceptable. I leave it the conscience of America to move our country beyond this debate and focus on issues of educational improvement.

Carolyn Getridge, Superintendent of Schools, Oakland Unified School District

Empathy humanizes human beings. It also catalyzes our humanity. Empathy fosters dialogical ways of being. Dialogical ways of being reflect existential and spiritual assumptions about human beings and our relations to each other. Specifically, dialogical communication assumes that human beings quest for completion, that human beings have the capacity to act deliberately upon the world, that human beings become human only through dialogical communication, that an existential and spiritual relation exists between human beings and the world, and that the world is unfinished (Buber, 1970; Cissna & Anderson, 1994; Freire, 1993). Dialogical communication positions us uniquely in our ability to bring forth the world through meaning creation and negotiation. Our becoming is entwined with that of the world. Anything that adversely affects our becoming also adversely affects the becoming of the world. Such ways of being reflect a deep sensitivity to human fragility. In this way, such ways of being aim to affirm life. According to Paulo Freire (1993):

Dialogue cannot exist . . . in the absence of a profound love for the world and people. The naming of the world, which is an act of creation and re-creation, is not possible if it is not infused with love. Love is at the same time the foundation of dialogue and dialogue itself. . . . On the other hand, dialogue cannot exist without humility. The naming of the world, through which people constantly re-create that world, cannot be an act of arrogance. . . . How can I dialogue if I am afraid of being displaced, the mere possibility causing me torment and weakness? . . . Dialogue further requires an intense faith in humankind, faith in their power to make and remake, to create and recreate, faith in their vocation to be more fully human. . . . Faith in people is an a priori requirement for dialogue. . . . Founding itself upon love, humility, and faith, dialogue becomes a horizontal relationship of which mutual trust between dialoguers is the logical consequence. (pp. 70-72)

Collins (1991) and Lorde (1984) also call for an emphasis on affirmation, empathy, and compassion to deal with our differences. Similarly, Pearce and Littlejohn (1997) contend that the transcendent discourse—which also stresses compassion and empathy—represents a superior means of negotiating moral conflict:

It can transform contempt into respect. It can minimize unreflective condemnation, and it can reduce violence. If we can see the rationality behind our opponent's position, we will no longer be able to characterize the opponent as insane, stupid, or misguided. When we realize the limits of our own philosophical assumptions, we will have more respect for the powers of our opponents' views. And, in the end, we will find the ability to disagree without silencing the other side through repression, injury and pain, or death. (p. 176)

Yet our ways of being reek of punishment and aggression. We are monological. We aid separation rather than union. The lack of compassion and empathy foster selfishness. Selfishness fosters deceit. In turn, deceit fosters distrust and suspicion. The result is that deceit obstructs the evolution of deep and meaningful human relations. The reaction to the school board was monological. It was devoid of any empathy for the endless number of urban children whose potential is being left untapped by poorly funded and managed urban educational systems. The reaction feigned concern for the children. It had to, as the context from which the reaction emerged was always devoid of empathy. It was never a matter of what harm Ebonics would do to the children. It was, rather, what harm Ebonics would to do to us. Consequently, never was any mention made throughout the controversy about the tremendous disparity in funding between urban and suburban schools. Neither was any mention made about the system used—local property taxes—to fund schools that make and sustain the disparity. Moreover, never was any mention made about the tiny fraction of the U.S. national budget allocated to education (5%) compared to the generous amount allocated to military spending (nearly 35% under Ronald Reagan). What moral argument can justify and defend such arrangements? It is the lack of any real interrogation of the status quo that compellingly shows our apathy and selfishness. This lack of interrogation reflects a quiet conspiracy among us to mask our hypocrisy. This kind of conspiracy characterizes peoples with monological ways of being. It allows us to claim a superior humanity without having to abandon our extant ways of being. We are spared the tribulations of acquiring new habits of being. We are also spared from having to contest the status quo and owning up to our complicity. Consequently, the nation just wanted the resolution stopped and the school board rebuked. It was tacitly understood that the controversy was to go no further.

POLITICS, ETHICS, ECONOMICS, AND AESTHETICS

To make Ebonics an educational priority for African American children is irresponsible at best and planned obsolescence at worst. Fluency in Ebonics is not an advantage in college admissions and employment.
 Earl G. Graves, Editor-in-Chief, Black Enterprise

Trust is foundational to dialogical communication. Paulo Freire (1993) writes, "Founding itself upon love, humility, and faith, dialogue becomes a horizontal relationship of which mutual trust between the dialoguers is the logical consequence. It would be a contradiction in terms if dialogue—loving, humble, and full of faith—did not produce this climate of mutual trust, which leads the dialoguers into ever close partnership in the naming of the world" (p. 72). Martin Buber (1994) writes about the lack of trust making for a crisis of communication:

The crisis of speech is bound up with this loss of trust in the closest possible fashion, for I can only speak to someone in the true sense of the term if I expect him to accept my word as genuine. Therefore, the fact that it is so difficult for present-day man to pray (note well: not to hold it to be true that there is a God, but to address Him) and the fact that it is so difficult for him to carry on a genuine talk with his fellow-men are elements of a single set of facts. This lack of trust in Being, this incapacity for unreserved intercourse with the other, points to an innermost sickness of the sense of existence. (p. 310)

This crisis of communication is now upon us as trust is rapidly disappearing from our everyday ways of being. A recent study by Harvard University School of Public Health reports that levels of trust have dropped precipitously over the last few decades (Morin & Balz, 1996). Our worldview also posits a deep distrust of our own humanity, of each other, of the world. No kind of existential connection is assumed between us and others. The result is discursive and material practices rife with distrust and suspicion. Prominent social scientists, such as Robert Axelrod (1984), now even claim that trust is unnecessary for functional human relations. All that is supposedly required is the threat of swift and potent retaliation.

Distrust is now institutionalized. This can be seen in the increasing deification of competition. We increasingly want competition to control all realms of being. We find an outpouring of scholarly theses extolling the virtues of competition. We hear about how competition ends discrimination. We hear about how competition allows for the productive expression of human aggression. We hear about how competition fosters fitness and produces socially responsible behavior. We hear that selfishness is good and greed even better. The Wall Street Journal tells us all of this again and again. Richard Dawkins of Oxford University and E. O. Wilson of Harvard, among many other distinguished scholars, all reason thusly.

Entering into dialogical communication is difficult. It challenges the constitution of our dominant consciousness. It demands a fundamental reorganization of fundamental assumptions about what being human means, thereby undermining the status quo. The elites of power and wealth will lose privileges. Dialogical communication ends competition. Cooperation transforms the distribution of wealth and resources. Dialogical communication also ends hierarchy and domination, as well as aggression, because trust fosters transparency and transparency blocks manipulation and domination. Dialogical communication exposes hierarchy as an artifact of dysfunctional communication.

The Wall Street Journal deflects criticisms of capitalism by pointing to the many heinous sins of other systems. It also successfully peddles a cheap understanding of democracy and entwines this understanding with capitalism. Democracy is conflated with capitalism. The Wall Street Journal also endorses the scholarly claim that competition and selfishness are in our genes. This viewpoint results in discussions only about ameliorating the negative outcomes of capitalism, such as dealing with the increasing gap between rich and poor, the increasing transfer of wealth from the bottom to the top, the management of rapidly depleting natural resources, and so forth. The focus is on finding a kinder and gentler version of capitalism: The legitimacy of capitalism avoids scrutiny. Historically, most critiques of the status quo posit no moral ground. On the other hand, political and social critiques have always been easy for The Wall Street Journal to dismiss. Yet, the fact remains that capitalism is exposed when human beings are seen as possessing existential and spiritual strivings. Without separation, capitalism crumbles. We thus need to focus on how capitalism thwarts union rather than simply on ameliorating what are commonly seen as the negative outcomes of capitalism.

In addition to fashioning our politics, ethics, and economics, our cosmology of separation also fashions our aesthetics. Our physical spaces seek to delimit human contact. Walls are ubiquitous. Buildings reflect a redundancy of right angles. Our spaces are hard and rigid. Our physical spaces also seek to maintain our differences and privileges, subtly yet powerfully conveying who belongs to what spaces. The rise of suburbs is born purely of separation. It shows us strenuously endeavoring to limit human contact. In this case, the ambition is to be separated from the different-looking peoples increasingly populating the urban world (Downs, 1998). However, the law no longer allows neighborhood associations to keep out such peoples. Many reports discuss race/ethnicity as a factor in suburban sprawl (Downs, 1998). The suburb is now giving way to the hypersuburb and the gated community as the different-looking peoples now descend on the suburbs. Legislators and planners are increasingly concerned as suburban sprawl now perilously taxes natural resources (Fairbanks, 1999; Gersh, 1996; Leinberger, 1998; Longman, 1998; Wen, 1999). We can only wonder what new spaces will be created when the different-looking peoples eventually descend on the hypersuburbs.

The nature of our spaces show us wanting to maintain separation. We want to live among peoples who appear like us. Another interesting feature of the suburbs are the grand spaces between the houses, the inward-facing housing, and the hidden entrances. Even within the suburbs separation pervades. The density of urban spaces undercuts this kind of separation. The result is that suburb and urban environments make for different human beings (Peirce, 1995; Poulson, 1997). The high density of the urban world forces us to confront the differences of others. We have to develop the temperaments, techniques, and skills to deal with such differences. We are also pushed to develop a temperament to deal with high levels of human density, the constant negotiation of endless relationships, all of which have to be carefully negotiated for practical purposes. The suburbs place no such demands on us. We are properly spaced to avoid any kind of meaningful human contact.

Suburbs undercut our capacity for union by thwarting the evolution of the temperaments and techniques vital to forging deep and meaningful relations with different peoples. Suburbs also limit the development of empathy and compassion by limiting contact with others less privileged. As a result, suburbs foster apathy and selfishness. We need only note the correlation between the rise of the suburbs and the death of liberal politics. The polls show again and again suburbans wanting an end to programs meant to help the disenfranchised and marginalized. Consequently, as federal policy is increasingly shaped by the suburban attitudes through voting patterns, I worry about the effects of this trend on a society that is becoming increasingly heterogenous and unequal. On the other hand, I know that the forces of separation will always be met by the forces of union. It is encouraging to hear reports of peoples returning to urban environments and others searching for developments that specifically focus on community (Wen, 1999). Also encouraging is the emergent trend in organizational design that emphasizes open spaces. However, both trends will remain the exception until a new consciousness emerges that ends separation.

SUMMARY AND CONCLUSION

Our deep distrust and suspicion of our humanity makes for a deep distrust of diversity. We have successfully legitimized this distrust of diversity. We have also developed the necessary mechanisms to sustain this legitimation. Our society thrives on the belief that institutions are vital to the evolution of the good society. It thrives on a deep distrust and suspicion of human beings. We have convinced ourselves that diversity threatens unity and social evolution. This kind of legitimation comes at a perilous cost, as it undermines both our civility and the potential of our humanity. To look at diversity as an artifact of union expands our understanding of diversity. Diversity as union gets us beyond diversity as differences. It gets us beyond the deep fears that the status quo thrives upon. Diversity as union also gives us a new vista from which to look at what being human means. It legitimizes a new politics and ethics.

A politics and ethics of separation needs rationales to justify separation. Rationales must be propagandized to justify the reifying of our fear and suspicion of differences, the unequal distribution of wealth, resources, and hierarchy. The Oakland controversy captures the playing out of such justifications. It also signals the commissioning of language and the decommissioning of race, ethnicity, class, and gender as the popular mechanism in which to pack our justifications. The Oakland controversy shows language as a superior mechanism that legitimizes a politics and ethics of separation. Language legitimizes our deep beliefs about race, class, and ethnicity without committing us to an open expression of such beliefs. The Oakland controversy also shows that language—by masking beliefs about race, class, and ethnicity—can forge new alliances bent on protecting and perpetuating the status quo. Traditional foes and victims have evolved to staunch defenders of the status quo. Rarely does a situation arises that reveals this weird transformation. With all this in mind, our attention now turns to a discussion of language.

3

The Nature
of Language

Ebonics is just another of those lies that's being taught to our young children and to America. First of all, our children are American, not Africans. Most of our children know nothing about the African continent. They don't know what country they're supposed to be from on that continent. . . . So what we have now is made-up English, slang, or whatever you want to call it, but it's made up. And now it is supposed to be for all African-American children. This is an insult to all blacks everywhere, but particularly to our children. It is the job of education to correct and teach, and not to promote this kind of garbage. That's just terrible.

Ezola Foster, Americans For Family Values

Ebonics . . . is a cruel joke. I believe that we have to, in this country, make it a point to see that our students . . . achieve proficiency in reading and writing and science and communicating, and we don't raise standards by lowering goals. We've got to be very clear about what we're saying. There is, within the larger African American community, and in other communities, various dialects. They're not languages, they are dialects. . . . We have to find ways to bridge out of that into proper English . . . but we should not be prepared to call it a second language or even a primary language.

Kweisi Mfume, President, NAACP

We're marginalizing our students. We're not asking for the best in them. Teachers are already faced with a lot of pressures in trying to educate these kids. We don't need to put an added burden on them by asking them to speak bad English.
   Armstrong Williams, Syndicated Columnist, *L.A. Times*

Ebonics has not been helpful to race relations. It brings out the worst thoughts if not the worst words from both black and white. Whites who defend ebonics as a second language, or even a place for it in the classroom, sound patronizing and condescending.
   Suzanne Fields, Columnist, *The Washington Times*

I am baffled by a lot of these statements that have come out without understanding any of the research that has been done on Ebonics, nor any appreciation of the way some children speak and the way it relates to African languages. What I'm seeing is a lot of shame . . . a lot of refusal to look at . . . what might be African about us. It's almost the same as when people used to call each other black . . . there's some shame to it.
   Cortland Malloy, Columnist, *Washington Post*

The reason why this has stirred up the hornet's nest it has is it's language being directly political; that it's language working as a political instrument, language allocating power. And one of the things that is an undercurrent here, being argued over, is whether speakers of black English have the right to use that language, whether their language has a legitimacy equal to that of standard white English.
   Robin Lakoff, Professor of Linguistics, University of California, Berkeley

I don't want to see another generation of black students be made to feel ashamed of their very rich home language.
   Ron Emmons, Assistant Professor, LA City College

Our relation to our languages is entwined with and reflects our relation to the world and each other. Thus when we change our relationship to each other we also change our relation to our languages. Our present dominant relation to our languages reflects ways of being that thwart our existential and spiritual strivings. As discussed earlier, the result is dysfunctionality, apathy, and disunity. A relation to language based on fear fosters and reflects human relations imbued with fear. Accordingly, to end the fear that shapes our relation to our languages requires ending the fear that burdens our relation to each other. I contend again that this fear springs from our deep distrust and suspicion of our humanity. We fear, as the Oakland controversy compellingly demonstrates, that the end of Standard English will bring chaos and disunity. We assume that human beings possess a proclivity for chaos. We look at Standard English and hierarchy as structures born of necessity to stop this proclivity. Consequently, evolved peoples supposedly have standardized languages and hierarchy.

Because the hegemony of the secular assumes that human beings have a proclivity for chaos and evil, it fosters human relations characterized by distrust, suspicion, and fear. In the case of the Oakland controversy, the fear is that too many languages threaten social chaos and disunity. Lurking behind the ruling is our supposed proclivity for chaos. Most opponents of the resolution view Ebonics as a threat to progress. Its fluidity is seen as a lack of rigor. Its lack of rigid and complex structures is seen as a defect. It is seen as merely expressive of our sensual selves, supposedly lacking the sophistication and rigor vital for progress.

In what follows I contend that a dialogical relation to the world and each other also changes our relation to our languages. Consequently, language diversity has no negative bearing on the forging of deep and meaningful relations. As always, I aim to show that the sentiments and criticisms that surround the Ebonics controversy spring from a deep and complex cultural, political, and social framework that legitimizes a politics and ethics of separation. I am committed to highlighting and critiquing the deep ideological structures that anchor this framework.

UNIVERSAL GRAMMAR

Now isn't it true that this [Ebonics] is a language with no verb conjugations, no vocabulary and no rules?
    Robert Novak, Host, CNN Crossfire

This is about as false a statement as one could make and one of the problems we have with black English or Ebonics is that we have all of these self-appointed experts who have not studied the language, who do not know anything about the language, haven't done any research, but yet they make all these claims about it that are totally false.
    Faye Vaughn-Cook, Chairman of Language and
    Communications, University of the District of Columbia

Not only is standard English not standard in the sense of being invariant from place to place, situation to situation, and oral medium to written medium; it also is not standard in the sense of representing an ideal against which to judge other dialects. Socio-linguistic studies show that all dialects have linguistic integrity. None is more regular than another. The features of [Black English] that contrast with standard English varieties are patterned and predictable, not random deviations. In other words, [Black English] is just as standardized as standard English-though it is not subject to prescription as is standard English.

  Carolyn Temple Adger, Center for Applied Linguistics

People used to believe that African American English was illogical, poorly constructed and inadequate for any cognitive or linguistic growth. . . . But while it is certainly different from Standard English, it is not inferior. The important question is: Is it systematic, regular and complex insofar as it involves a vocabulary or lexicon, a phonology or sound system, and a grammar and a set of rules? Black English meets these requirements.

  John R. Rickford, Linguist, Department of Linguistics, Stanford University

There is no such thing as black English. . . . There is standard English and substandard, proper usage and improper. . . . It is condescending—indeed, racist—to suggest that black children cannot or should not speak standard English all the time.

  Les Payne & Cynthia Tucker, *NABJ Journal*

Black English is a dialect. . . . It's black people shooting themselves in the foot. They're [the school board] implying that black people are incapable of learning a language which is so close to theirs that it's not a different language.

  John McWhorter, Professor of Linguistics and African American Studies, University of California, Berkeley

First and foremost, there is no reason to think there needs to be a linguistic norm. As Chomsky has noted, "Communication is a more-or-less matter, seeking a fair estimate of what the other person said and has in mind" (*Language and Thought*, p. 21). I can understand some speakers of Ebonics roughly as well as I can understand my fourteen-year-old nephew, but I can understand neither as well as I can understand people with whom I have much common background and shared knowledge. People of different linguistic communities communicate effectively when they need or want to do so. There is no reason to force a standard upon them in advance, as we try to do in the U.S.

The only reason it may appear that we need a norm is that we have a particular kind of society in which socio-economic status is denied to groups which are historically disadvantaged (people of color, or people who did not pay attention in high school, or did not go to college), and the way they speak identifies what group they belong to. It's true that we could continue to try to change people so that they have a chance of doing well within this corrupt system, but our energies might be better spent in trying to change the system itself and in heralding the linguistic talents of the communities most threatened by authority figures.

Jeff MacSwan, Lecturer, Postdoctoral Fellow, Linguistics Department, UCLA

Ebonics is not just a bit of amateur crackpotism. It is professional crackpotism, well within the pedagogical mainstream. . . . The Oakland School District can point to a rich corpus of academic work on which to base its decision.

Jacob Heilbrunn, *The New Republic*

To contest the hegemony of Standard English is to contest bedrock assumptions that undergird our popular understanding of language. It is also to contest popular conceptions about the origin of language. The hegemony of Standard English assumes that human beings have a proclivity for social devolution and animality that hierarchy limits and that communication and language are artifacts of necessity. This is the dominant thesis on the origin of language. It is assumed that the origins of communication and language can be found in apes, bonobos, and chimpanzees. The differences between us and such animals are popularly assumed to be quantitative rather than qualitative. Consequently, many researchers look to such animals to understand the nature and origins of communication and language. Ann James Premack and David Premack (1991) explain:

Why try to teach human language to an ape? In our case the motive was to better define the fundamental nature of language. It is often said that language is unique to the human species. Yet it is now well known that many other animals have elaborate communication systems of their own. It seems clear that language is a general system of which human language is a particular, albeit remarkably refined, form. Indeed, it is possible that certain features of human language that are considered to be uniquely human belong to the more general system, and that these features can be distinguished from those that are unique to the human information-processing regimes. If, for example, an ape can be taught the rudiments of human language, it should clarify the dividing line between the general system and the human one. (p. 16)

In *The Ape That Spoke: Language and Evolution of The Human Mind,* John McCrone (1991) posits that our language facility has origins in our supposed ape ancestry, and language is made for a self-conscious mind. He writes, "It may be an obvious statement, but the human mind must have evolved. It cannot have sprung fully formed from nowhere, turning a dull-witted ape into a glowingly self-conscious human being. The mind must have been shaped over time by the same evolutionary pressures that made man walk on two legs" (p. 12). The evolution was supposedly catalyzed by apes moving from forests to grasslands. This forced movement—as a result of the deterioration of the lush forest habitat—brought about a need for superior mechanisms to afford coordination and cooperation. According to McCrone (1991), "Language provided the building material with which evolution could write revolutionary new software for the hardware of the ape brain" (p. 48). He theorizes that language evolved gradually over thousands of years and that this evolution led to new social behaviors. In turn, the evolution of new behaviors led to the further evolution of language. He writes, "One change would feed rapidly into the other, until one day man would have found himself with full-blown speech and a richly developed culture" (p. 159). The evolution of language supposedly led to the expansion of our cognitive capacity. Leslie Aiello (1998) writes, "One certain thing is that the evolution of increased social intelligence would be closely linked with the evolution of language. The reason for this is simply that an increased ability to communicate symbolically would be tied with the increased ability to cheat" (p. 31).

In a paper titled *The Origin of Language and Cognition,* Ib Ulbaek (1998) contends that language actually evolved from animal cognition rather than from animal communication. It supposedly "grew out of cognitive systems already in existence and working: it formed a communicative bridge between already-cognitive animals" (p. 33). Ulbaek also believes that evolutionary forces catalyzed the rise of language. It evolved for informational purposes so as to afford superior coordination and cooperation. Ulbaek posits that it is our evolved ability to transact complex codes that distinguish us from apes. Supposedly, apes escaped the harsh grassland environments that pushed the rest of us to develop the cognitive capacity that led to the evolution of language. We, on the other hand, supposedly had no choice. We had to develop language. It is the nature of genes to do whatever is necessary to survive, natural selection theory posits. The evolution of language was also supposedly pushed along by the need to develop both quicker modes of transmission and superior ways of deceiving others so as to maximize our chances of surviving and thriving in an environment hostile to life.

Mortensen (1991) posits that language, communication, and culture coevolved to end the violent conflict that results from our supposed capacity for strife and conflict. He also sees communication and language as artifacts of necessity. Both evolved out of the need for coordination so as to establish relations with others—either for protection or acquisition of resources, alliances, and mates—that are necessary for our survival. Both also evolved out of the need for manipulation in order to increase our chances of survival. Mortensen (1991) explains:

> It is not difficult, therefore, to privilege the possibility that our ancestors acted under communal pressures to devise primitive codes that worked well enough (in a communal sense) to insure a measure of territorial control required to gather food and capture objects of prey as well as facilitate the evasion of other predators. It seems plausible that those synchronized forms of expressive activity that were exhibited during episodes of procreation, food gathering, and predatory encounter would have contributed to the acquisition of additional skills in the production and maintenance of access to vital sources of sustenance—air, sun, water, heat, food, and shelter—as well as to longer term cooperation in establishing sites for food quests, the killing of large prey, and the use of organic resources to produce more effective tools and weapons of collective self-defense. In such a rich ecological circumstance the fundamental discovery would have been a conceptual plan to talk or gesture one's way in or out of a state of war or peace with other living things. (p. 286)

Mortensen sees communication as a tool, an artifact of necessity, something secular, *of* human beings. No spiritual relation supposedly exists between being, communication, and language. Supposedly, neither communication nor language performs any *sacred* function. Daniel Dennett (1995) also posits that communication, language, and culture are artifacts of natural selection forces. He writes, "What is preserved and transmitted in cultural evolution is informational—in a media-neutral, language-neutral sense" (pp. 353-354). Dennett posits a transmission view of communication, language, and culture. He also assumes an informational view of communication. This view is pervasive in different scholarly literatures. Kenichi Aoki (1991) also traces the origins of *cultural transmission* in our evolutionary machinations. He defines cultural transmission as "the transfer of information between individuals by social learning" (p. 439). Moreover, "Cultural transmission is not limited to the human (e.g., the songs of most perching birds are culturally transmitted), but it is particularly important in our species. Without it, there would be no language(s); there would be no toolmaking tradition(s); civilization as we know it would not exist" (p. 440).

A distinguished group of primatologists and zoologists now claim that the last point of differentiation between human beings and animals has now been empirically resolved: Both are cultural beings. It was recently prominently reported that chimpanzees show cultural variation ("Chimps Exhibit . . . Humanness, Study Finds"). Stephen Jay Gould (1999) editorialized in *The New York Times* that this latest news is really no surprise: "Why are we so surprised by such a finding? The new documentation is rich and decisive—but why would anyone have doubted the existence of culture in chimps, given well-documented examples in other examples and our expanding knowledge of the far more sophisticated mental lives of chimpanzees." Frans de Waal (1999) writes about the research to which Gould refers: "The record is so impressive that it will be difficult to keep these apes out of the cultural domain without once again moving the goalposts" (p. 635). According to Whiten et al. (1999), authors of the recent research, "a cultural behavior is one that is transmitted repeatedly through social or behavioral learning to become a population-level characteristic. By this definition, cultural differences . . . are well established phenomena in the animal kingdom and are maintained through a variety of social transmission mechanisms" (p. 682). Whiten et al. contend that this is an inclusive definition of culture. It rejects language as the defining element of culture. Whiten et al. posit that many opponents of natural selection theory use language to constrain culture as a uniquely human phenomenon. It is what Frans de Waal refers to as "moving the goalposts."

Many linguists also contend that language must have natural selection origins. In a recent compilation of twenty-four essays on the origin of language, *Approaches To The Evolution Of Language*, Michael Studdert-Kennedy and the other editors of the book said the following: "What is needed . . . is a more subtle view of evolving human society in which the capacity to speak and listen . . . might afford an individual, male or female, and its close kin a selective advantage over conspecific rivals in forming coalitions, discussing plans of action, and otherwise negotiating a path to higher social status, and so to more successful feeding and mating" (1988, pp. 3-4). According to Chris Knight (1998), also an editor of this recent compilation, "Darwinism is setting a new research agenda across the related fields of palaeoanthropology, evolutionary psychology and theoretical linguistics. . . . It is now widely accepted that no other theoretical framework has equivalent potential to solve the major outstanding problems in human origins research" (p. 68). Most of the contributors shared Knight's view. For example, Robert Worden (1998) writes, "A theory of language evolution should be consistent with the neo-Darwinian theory of evolution. . . . Therefore we should look for theories in which language did not arise de novo in the human brain, but is based in pre-existing animal cognitive faculties" (pp. 150-151). He argues that language is an outgrowth of primate social intelligence. The common assumption throughout the book is that language is informational.

A transmission view of communication, language, and culture commonly assumes a secular epistemology. This way of looking at the world assumes that a world exists outside of us that is reducible and knowable. It also assumes the possibility of separation of the observer from the observed, the knower from the known. It seeks explanations devoid of metaphysical and religious components, and empirically verifiable through observation. Such explanations must also be devoid of cultural values, beliefs, and assumptions. Explanations must also be atemporal, acontextual, and apolitical. In addition, this secular epistemology posits that set rules are observable in both human behavior and nature, and empirical observation of these rules is definitive. It looks to the language of science as a framework of clarity and precision. The aim is for language to reflect an objective reality (Lincoln & Guba, 1985; Reinharz, 1988). It must strive to correspond with reality and symbols must accurately represent things. Supposedly, answers to the deepest problems are derived by giving further thought to the nature of language. This secular epistemology assumes that nature is objectifiable and knowable, and a dichotomy exists between subject and object. According to Dervin (1980), "The idea here is that the world can be seen as discoverable, describable and predictable and the purpose of information [communication, language] is to describe it and predict it" (p. 89).

A representational view of communication, language, and culture emerges. It is popularly assumed that supposedly complex languages reflect complex peoples who have achieved complex and sophisticated understandings of the world. The result is the association of peoples with supposedly complex languages with complex cultures. Conversely, peoples with supposedly less evolved languages—or associated racially or ethnically with any—are commonly seen as less evolved and of backward and primitive cultures. In this view, different cultures reflect different levels of evolution and progress. Yet this bedrock assumption of transmission that undergirds popular understandings of communication, language, and culture undermines our understanding of what being human means. A transmission view of communication and culture masks the complexity that constitutes human interaction and motivation. Communication is about the creation and negotiation of shared meaning. It is fundamentally a relational rather than an informational process. Through communication human beings develop relations with the world and each other. We are humanized through communication. Therefore, communication always transcends our relations with each other. Communication entwines us with the world; it is always positioning and framing us in a relation to the world. Simply put, rather than representational—that is, epistemological—communication is ontological. Consequently, cultures, too, are ontological. Cultures exist within us and through us. As Lee Thayer (1997) accurately observes:

> A culture . . . is comprised of all of those means by which we mystify ourselves. Mind, therefore, is something more than merely internalized culture, and culture is something more than merely externalized mind. That something more is that they are the same thing, and the trick of language, of communication, is to make them appear to us to be separate things, so that we can pretend to an innocence long lost to us, in the same way that the trick of language, of communication, is to make the knower and the known appear to us to be separate things, so that we can pretend to be innocent of both. (p. 8)

The ontological nature of culture explains why all cultures known to anthropologists posit a spiritual dimension. This is the defining relation of all cultures. It is our relation to the world that mediates our relation to each other and even to ourselves. A representational view of communication, language, and culture misses this reality by downplaying the universality of our *spiritualness*. It becomes easy to view cultures as simply about the transmission of learned behaviors. Implicitly, such a view reinforces the belief that human beings are aspiritual beings—with, again, no real distinction from, say, chimpanzees and apes. Culture is reduced to a network of learned behaviors rather than a set of complex relationships revolving recursively around understandings of the world.

Cultures are born of our questing to bring meaning to bear on the world. Values, beliefs, assumptions, and so forth organically belong to cultures, communication, and relationships. Cultures show our *connectedness* to the world. The meanings derived from our questing recursively fashion our relations to each other. Consequently, cultures that posit a hierarchical ordering of society also posit a hierarchical ordering of the world. It is the questing to understand the world that makes culture a uniquely human phenomenon. To view culture as merely behavioral modification, as primatologists and zoologists do, masks the spiritual dimension of culture and reduces the complexity of what being human means. The task is for Gould and company to show chimpanzees questing to understand the cosmos. This matter has nothing to do with elevating the status of human beings. This kind of hierarchy, after all, is purely a social construction. It is a matter of genuinely trying to understand what being human means and the nature of the world.

Scholars are increasingly calling attention to the spiritual element of communication (e.g., Chase, 1993; Clair, 1998; Gonzalez, 1998; Goodall, 1993; Kirkwood, 1993; Long, 1997; McPhail, 1996; Ohlhauser, 1996; Pokora, 1996; Witmer, 1997). Turkey (1990) contends that communication theorists "consider no dimension other than the mental, social and biological—in short, only the secular. What contemporary theories ignore is human spirituality and its possible role in human communication" (p. 66). Smith (1993) argues that communication scholars have "assiduously [avoided] talking about the non-material elements of communication" (p. 267). The result is that a secular hegemony pervades communication theory and inquiry that circumscribes certain notions about what being human means, our relations to each other, and our relation to the world. According to Smith (1993), "The problem with ignoring the spiritual is that we cannot deepen our theory nor advance our understanding of the art of rhetoric without investigating the spiritual dimension" (p. 268). Chase (1993) writes, "Rethinking human communication by recognizing the fundamental experience of obligation for the Other provides an exciting framework by which one can challenge the recurring . . . practices of everyday life which produce and reproduce a disregard for the social, material, and spiritual well-being of people, as well as a disregard for the service due a transcendent Spiritual Being" (p. 14). Long (1997) believes that a spiritual perspective "with regard to communication research allows us to go beyond the transmission mode of communicating to re-embody a more complex knowing and relationships with others and ourselves" (pp. 9-10). As for language, Wilhelm von Humbolt, writing over a century ago, and whose writings on language remain helpful to linguists, argued that the origin of language is spiritual:

> Language is deeply entangled in the spiritual evolution of mankind. . . . Language, indeed, arises from a depth of human nature which everywhere forbids us to regard it as a true product and creation of peoples. It possesses an autonomy that visibly declares itself to us, though inexplicable in its nature, and, seen from this aspect, is no production of activity, but an involuntary emanation of the spirit, no work of nations, but a gift fallen to them by their inner destiny. (p. 24)

Noam Chomsky (1968), undoubtedly the most distinguished linguist of this century, contends that language is uniquely human. He forcefully rejects the natural selection theory view of the origin of language. He sees human beings as being uniquely programmed and equipped for language. In *Language and Mind*, Chomsky (1968) writes:

Anyone concerned with the study of human nature and human capacities must somehow come to grips with the fact that all normal human beings acquire language, whereas acquisition of even its barest rudiments is quite beyond the capacities of an otherwise intelligent ape. . . . It is widely thought that the extensive modern studies of animal communication challenge this classical view; and it is almost universally taken for granted that there exists a problem of explaining the *evolution* of language from systems of animal communication. However, a careful look at recent studies of animal communication seems to me to provide little support for these assumptions. Rather, these studies bring out even more clearly the extent to which human language appears to be a unique phenomenon, without significant analogue in the animal world. If this is so, it is quite senseless to raise the problem of explaining the evolution of human language from more primitive systems of communication that appear at lower levels of cognitive capacity. (p. 59)

Chomsky (1988) contends all languages follow a fixed set of universal principles of language structure that are biologically determined. As a result, language differences are cultural rather than biological. According to Chomsky:

My own work leads me to the conclusion that there are far reaching, deep-seated universal principles of language structure. I think we tend to be unaware of them and pay attention only to differentiation of languages because of a very natural response to variety as distinct from the essential shared properties on mankind. . . . I think we will discover that language structures really are uniform. The uniformity results from the existence of fixed, immutable, biologically determined principles, which provide the schematism which makes a child capable of organizing and coming to terms with his rather restricted experiences of everyday life and creating complex intellectual structures on that basis. (pp. 151-152)

Chomsky labels this underlying calculus a *Universal Grammar.* In my view, this calculus could also be described as an *attractor*—a self-organizing calculus that exists within all living systems. Attractors give systems symmetry and diversity. They noncoercively allow the system to take on endless possible variations. In this way, rather than limiting, attractors enable. According to Chomsky:

I think in a general way we can say that a person's knowledge of his language is based on a system of rules and principles. If you look carefully at these rules, you will discover that the rules themselves are of a narrow range. There are certain kinds of rules that are permissible; there are other kinds of rules that are not permissible. There are also strict conditions on their application. (p. 152)

David Lightfoot (1999) writes, "There seems to be nothing in other species remotely comparable to the kind of computations and compositionality made available by the human UG [Universal Grammar]" (p. 229). He also forcefully reports that the historical record offers no proof of languages being anything but enormously complex. Derek Bickerton (1995) is equally adamant about the equality of languages: "If there were any link between cultural complexity and linguistic complexity, we would expect to find that the most complex societies had the most complex languages while simpler societies had simpler languages. We do not find any such thing. . . . When you take all aspects into account, languages are roughly equal in complexity" (p. 35). In short, no language has ever been shown to be less complex than others. About the origin of language, Jean-Jacques Rousseau (1986) writes, "Conventional language belongs to man alone. That is why man makes progress in good as well as in evil, and why animals do not. This single distinction seems to be far reaching. They say that it can be explained by a difference in organs. I should be curious to see that explanation" (p. 244). He believes that language origins can be found in human passions.

Chomsky's position on the origin of language was criticized by many of the contributors in the compilation of essays by James Hurford and company. David Lightfoot was also criticized. The notion that the origin of language can be anything other than an artifact of natural selection forces was never given any kind of consideration. The contributors speculated about how natural selection theory can account for the origin of language. Many different and even conflicting scenarios were offered. Yet, no contributor pointed to a less evolved and complex language. It would seem that such languages would have had to exist. But the real problem is how the contributors casually assumed that language must have natural selection origins. It is apparently unfathomable that such an explanation can remain a mystery of the world. It is equally unfathomable that language can have existential and spiritual origins. Supposedly, language represents the evolution of human communication. Communication is artifact of cognitive processes. It, too, is informational. Language is seen the defining feature of communication. Accordingly, the origins and nature of language supposedly explain communication.

Implicit in the notion that language evolved from gestures is that communication is about our capacity to deal with symbols and codes. Natural selection theorists posit that the rise of language is associated with increased cognitive capacity. This notion lingers deep in our consciousness. We do assess—as the Oakland controversy compellingly shows—others by language use and vocabulary size. We even have institutional tests that supposedly make such assessments accurately. Indeed, such assessments have real consequences, as the Oakland controversy compellingly shows. Children who are assessed with less language facility are commonly assumed to have cognitive problems and are labeled learning impaired. The research shows that black and poor children suffer this fate disproportionately.

The association of cognitive complexity with the ability to manipulate symbols and codes resides deep within our consciousness and permeates our ethics and politics. But communication has really nothing much to do with language; language is but one artifact of communication. Communication is about meaning, specifically about the negotiation and creation of meaning. Communication precedes and exceeds language. It is communication—through our questing to understand the cosmos—that pushes, stretches, and bends language. It is meaning that makes for the evolution of new symbols and codes. It is meaning that makes for communication when common symbols and codes are nonexistent between peoples. It is our proclivity and capacity for meaning creation rather than our language facility that makes us uniquely human.

To look at language as communication also gives us no way of framing what human beings do. Such a position assumes that language and communication are fundamentally artifacts of cognitive processes. It gives us no way of dealing with the rich mystical schemes of the world that all peoples develop. What, again, becomes the explanations for the universality of spirituality? What becomes of our quest to understand and establish a relation with a nonphysical world? What explains the origins of the apparent nonphysical and noncognitive uses of communication? Knight and company express no concern with such matters. To look at language and communication as artifacts either of cognitive processes or necessity assumes that nothing is really *sacred* about communication. No spiritual relation is assumed between communication and being or between us and the world. Knight and company focus on the neurobiological origins and mechanics of language. Reductionism is their chosen path to understanding language and communication. John L. Locke (1998) speculates thusly: "It thus appears that humans have a mechanism in the brain that controls sound-making, possibly operating in some isolation from other mechanisms that are needed for vocabulary acquisition or grammar. If one were to look for this mechanism, neurosurgical and neuropathological findings suggest that a good place to start would be the Supplementary Motor Area (SMA), a structure that is located in the frontal lobes, along the mesial surface of the superior frontal lobes" (p. 193). Communication rejects reductionism; meaning springs from relationships, is constituted relationally, and materializes only through relationships. No origin really exists. Our proclivity for meaning transcends cognitive processes. It shows us reaching for the world rather than merely concerned with coordinating tasks, acquiring resources, and other such secular functions. What emerges is a phenomenon that is as much metaphysical as existential.

But why this need to know exactly the origin of language and communication? What would proving the origin of language do for us? We seem curiously fixated with proving our animal origins. Marshall Sahlins (1976) contends that Western peoples are the only peoples known to anthropologists who claim such origins. Other peoples consistently claim an origin in a spiritual entity. Neither the editors nor the contributors of *Approaches To The Evolution Of Language* tell us what the rewards are of knowing the origins of language. Yet, all the contributors offer different and conflicting scenarios about the origin of language. It seems a matter of our being simply bent on having the world yield to our techniques. Nothing will be allowed to remain a mystery. We will dissect and do whatever we can to unlock the secrets of the world. It is all a reflection of our conviction that with the correct epistemology and techniques human beings can attain dominion over the world. We show no interest in the ethics and politics that flow from this kind of conviction.

Stephen Jay Gould (1999) contends that our unwillingness to accept our animal origins is simply about ego. He asks us to make peace with the emergent findings:

> We are linked to chimpanzees . . . by complete chains of intermediate forms that proceed backward from our current state into the fossil record until the two lineages meet in a common ancestor. But all these intermediate forms are extinct, and the evolutionary gap between modern humans and chimps therefore stands as absolute and inviolate. In this crucial genealogical sense all humans share equal fellowship as members of Homo sapiens. In biological terms, with species defined by historical and genealogical connection, the most mentally deficient among us is as fully human as Einstein. (p. A4)

But Gould misdiagnoses the matter. The matter has nothing to do with trying to put down apes and chimpanzees so as to raise the status of human beings. I have absolutely no problem with a theory of evolution. I also have no qualms about overlaps existing or common threads being found in all manifestations of life. In my view, life is a relational phenomenon and all manifestations of life function relationally. The point I am trying to make is that the scholarly community distorts what being human means through an epistemology that obliterates the complexity that constitutes our humanness. The problem is that Gould and company flagrantly disregard any other explanation that even hints of spiritual or existential notions. The problem is the insistence that human beings *must* have evolved from chimpanzees. The problem is also about downplaying the complexity of human beings. In *Language and Human Behavior*, Derek Bickerton (1995) puts the matter well:

> The claim that we are just another species ignores the range as well as the power of human behavior. The range of behavior in other creatures does not extend much beyond seeking food, seeking sex, rearing and protecting young, resisting predation, grooming, fighting rivals, exploring and defending territory, and unstructured play. Human beings do all these things, of course, but they also do math, tap dance, engage in commerce, build boats, play chess, invent novel artifacts, drive vehicles, litigate, draw representationally, and do countless other things that no other species ever did. Any theory that would account for human behavior has to explain why the behavior of all other species is, relatively speaking, so limited, while that of one single species should be so broad. Why is there not a continuum of behaviors, growing gradually from amoeba to human? Why don't chimpanzees build boats, why can't orangutans tap dance? (p. 6)

The problem is also the stridency of the belief that human beings can possibly have no other business with the world. Moreover, it is the disregard of all research that shows us being distinctively different. I reject how organized religion and spirituality have been conflated, so that the *sins* of religion are now the sins of spirituality, and how any hint of spirituality is seen as subordinating truth to mysticism. Finally, I reject how Gould and company can speculate about the nature of the world without suffering the contempt that others who posit nonsecular explanations attract. I reject this kind of *disciplining* power that both Gould and natural-selection theory enthusiasts possess. Most of the academics view beliefs as having no redeeming scholarly purposes. Beliefs are seen as interfering with the ambition to produce hard truths—truths that can withstand objective scrutiny. Yet, beliefs by no means undercut our capacity to understand the world. The problem is with *our relation* to our beliefs. Beliefs allow us to understand without knowing by releasing understanding from knowing. Also, beliefs allow us to hope, to have faith, to leap beyond the present. In this way, beliefs have the potential to expand our understanding of the cosmos, thus expanding the potential of human action.

To view human beings aexistentially and aspiritually reinforces the belief that human beings have no moral claim on liberation. We are, according to E. O. Wilson (1978) and Richard Dawkins (1989), merely survival machines doing the business of our selfish genes. Supposedly, the mission of life is survival through manipulation and competition; we have no other business with the world or with each other. Yet Knight and company have made—by any standard—no compelling case that our capacity for language is an artifact of natural selection forces. For certain, Knight and company err egregiously in conflating language with communication.

I offer no specifics on the origins of language. I am comfortable for now with leaving the matter a mystery; I even find the ambiguity of the matter enlivening. What I do find fascinating is the nature of language. No one disputes the validity of Universal Grammar. I am, however, really concerned with the ethics and politics that flow from the claims that Knight and company make. I am concerned with how such claims legitimize the status quo and, consequently, legitimize the forces of domination and oppression. In this case, grand speculations and specious theoretical schemes have disastrous and debilitating consequences. This is why I have addressed the subject of the origin of language. Rather than seeking to thwart any kind of inquiry, I am simply arguing that Knight and company need to heed the political consequences of Charles Darwin's natural selection theory. This theory is increasingly being used to justify selfishness, competition, greed, discrimination, and hierarchy. On the other hand, I have also sought to release us from the claims and assumptions that Knight and company make. This release is vital so as to get beyond the status quo. We are released enough to consider new conceptions of what being human means.

Universal Grammar makes the acquisition of any number of languages relatively easy. Its plasticity fosters diversity. Consequently, children tend to have no real difficulty acquiring a number of languages. Universal Grammar organically constrains language differences. The result is the possibility for endless articulations of the world—reflecting the rich and fecund nature of the world—without any threat of disunity and chaos. Universal Grammar releases us from the assumption that diversity threatens unity and it assumes that human beings possess a natural proclivity for diversity. As Robert Torrance (1994) astutely observes, "Language not only frees man from the immediacy of the actual by its openness to diversity and adaptability to change, but gives direction to our freedom by evoking an indeterminate future goal for our actions and guiding us conditionally in quest of its penultimate realization" (p. 49). It seems, as Wilhelm von Humboldt suggested long ago, that to know the nature of language is to know something about the nature of God.

MODES AND RHEOMODES

Giving faulty English official status, accentuates the negative, disrespects the positive, and ushers the children into a world of excusemaking, false expectations, and to a world of justifiable rejection.
    Editorial, *Tennessee Tribune*

We do not support the teaching of Ebonics. We support the teaching of good, standard English.
    Paul Vallas, Director, Chicago Public Schools

We're going to recognize that there are these language patterns and we're going to do something about it. We want all of our students to speak Standard English.
    Maxine Waters, D-CA, U.S. Representative

Tell us, this is not what's being done. That we will now validate the language of Snoop Doggy Dog, and the language that's been used to denigrate women, to bring profanity, and violent written language into our homes. Somebody someplace is about to validate this language and say this is a reflection of us and how we speak, this is the be all and end all of all of us. We won't hear it.
    Cojo Nomde, Host, WHMM

Our underserved young people do not lack a facility for language. On the contrary, they are masters of linguistic improvisation. With relatively few resources available to them in their schools and communities, their language continues to be a defining element of personal style and creativity. So it can't help our children to be told at every utterance that their mode of expression—which is intimately linked to their identity—is wrong, wrong, wrong.
    Khephra Burns, *Essence*

David Bohm, considered by many to be one of the foremost theoretical physicists of this century and who theorized about the constraints and destructiveness of languages that engender fragmentation, believes that an emergent language mode is necessary to complement emergent understandings of the world. Such understandings point to a world of consciousness. All of the world belongs and evolves from consciousness. Consciousness depicts a world that ebbs and flows and it undermines the notion that the world is fixed, constant, and mechanical. It also delegitimizes the validity of dualisms, such as that between forces and matter. Instead, our ways of understanding and speaking about the world must have the capacity to ebb and flow to the natural rhythms of the world. Bohm believes that our emergent language mode must be verb driven and without any kind of stridency that blocks spontaneity.

Bohm acknowledges that the possibility of an entirely new language mode is unlikely. He believes that what is provisionally possible is a new language mode that shifts the focus to the verb and away from the noun. He calls this new mode the *rheomode* (from the Greek word *rheo* "to flow"). In *Wholeness and the Implicate Order*, Bohm (1980) contends that the rheomode stresses fluidity rather than rigidity:

> We will now consider a mode in which movement is to be taken as primary in our thinking and in which this notion will be incorporated into the language structure by allowing the verb rather than the noun to play a primary role. . . . [T]he rheomode will be an experiment in the use of language, concerned mainly with trying to find out whether it is possible to create a new structure that is not so prone toward fragmentation as is the present one. Evidently, then, our inquiry will have to begin by emphasizing the role of language in shaping our overall world views as well as in expressing them. (pp. 30-31)

Bohm contends that the fragmentation reflected by our common mode of language originates with a worldview, presently the dominant one—that holds to fragmentary notions—such as gender, race, causes and effects, forces and matter, and so forth—of the world:

> [T]he dominant form of subject-verb-object tends continually to lead to fragmentation; and it is evident that the attempt to avoid this fragmentation by skillful use of other features of the language can work only in a limited way, for, by force of habit, we tend sooner or later, especially in broad questions concerning our overall world views, to fall unwittingly into the fragmentary mode of functioning implied by the basic structure. The reason for this is not only that the subject-verb-object form of language is continually implying an inappropriate division between things but, even more, that the ordinary mode of language tends very strongly to take its own function for granted, and thus it leads us to concentrate almost exclusively on the content under discussion, so that little or no attention is left for the actual symbolic function of the language itself. (p. 31)

Standard English reflects our need for complex and rigid structures so as to suppress and control our supposed proclivity for chaos. We also want our languages—in this case, Standard English—to control and order the supposedly random forces of the world. We want subordination. We want our languages to reflect a mechanical and secular world. We have deliberately sought a relation that undercuts creativity, diversity, and spontaneity. We fear that social chaos will occur without our language being rigid and complex. Consequently, our dominant relation to language and communication is devoid of fun and joy. It lacks any vitality to ebb and flow to the natural rhythms of the world. It retards our cognitive and sensual development by stressing subordination rather than creation. It debilitates us by reifying a deep fear of ourselves, each other, and the world. It is legitimized by the mistaken notion that communication, language, and culture are about messages, symbols, and signs. Instead, all are about relationships. As Chomsky (1968) aptly explains:

> Men do not understand one another by actually exchanging signs for things, nor by mutually occasioning one another to produce exactly and completely the same concept; they do it by touching in one another the same link in the chain of their sensory ideas and internal conceptualizations, by striking the same note on their mental instruments, whereupon matching but not identical concepts are engendered in each other. Only within these limits, and with these divergences, do they come together on the same word. In naming the commonest of objects, such as a horse, they all mean the same animal, but each attaches to the word a different idea, more sensuous or more rational, more vivid than a thing, or nearer to the dead sign, and so on. (p. 152)

The point is that emergent understandings of the world call forth an emergent relation to communication, language, and culture. Distinct about such a relation is the subordination of symbols to meanings. It is devoid of the fear that makes for the stridency that engenders reification and alienation. We find no aspiration to use language to bring order upon a supposedly random world, or to mirror an objective world. The end of reification and alienation allows for the flexibility and spontaneity vital for us to ebb and flow with the consciousness of the world. An emergent relation to communication, language, and culture assumes that the world is laden with potentiality.

Our language proclivity is catalyzed by our existential and spiritual strivings to bring meaning to bear on the world and our striving for union. It is also catalyzed by the potential of the world that is constantly trying to unfold. The goal is always creation. As Jacques Ellul (1994) explains, to look at language as merely about information misses the existential and relational potential of human interaction. Such an understanding greatly impoverishes our relationships by emasculating our intertwinedness:

The blessed uncertainty of language is the source of all its richness. I do not know exactly how much of my message the other person hears, how he interprets it, or what he will retain of it. I know that a kind of electric current is established between us; words penetrate him, and I have the feeling that he either reacts positively or else rejects what I have said. I can interpret his reaction, and then the relationship will rebound, accompanied by a rich halo of overtones. He does not understand, and I see that. So I speak again, weaving another piece of cloth, but this time with a different design. I come up with what I think will reach him and be perceived by him. The uncertainty of meaning and the ambiguity of language inspire creativity. (pp. 122-123)

The end of ambiguity correlates with the end of diversity. Ambiguity vitalizes communication. It keeps meanings open and uncertain, thereby allowing meanings to have the flexibility and spontaneity to ebb and flow to the natural rhythms of the world. In keeping our meanings open, ambiguity also keeps us open to the world and allows for the possibility of new and different meanings. It exercises our capacity to bring meaning to bear upon the world.

I make a distinction between ambiguity and uncertainty. I believe that most scholars err in using the terms interchangeably. I define ambiguity as any relation that is pregnant with the possibility for infinite meaning. The underlying assumption is that all the possible meanings are unknown. Our relation to the world is ambiguous. Our relation to the future is ambiguous. Uncertainty, on the other hand, is any relation with the possibility of finite meaning. The underlying assumption is that all the possible meanings are known. Illness, for example, is about uncertainty. Our condition can either improve or deteriorate. Uncertainty is an artifact of ambiguity. What is compelling about this emergent distinction between ambiguity and uncertainty is that it foregrounds the relational nature of being human, foremost of which is our relation to the world. Foregrounding the relational nature of being human allows us to understand uncertainty and ambiguity as relational phenomena.

What is useful about this relational way of looking at ambiguity and uncertainty is the recognition that any relation that is either ambiguous or uncertain can be changed. It is simply a matter of altering the discursive, performative, and communicative practices that constitute the relation in a particular way. The goal of wanting to do so could be merely to change the meaning options that either an ambiguous or uncertain relation presents us with. This can be potentially useful for persons who face a dreaded set of meaning options. We may even want to transfer an uncertain relation to an ambiguous one so as to release ourselves from a limited set of meaning options. Any relation can be reconfigured. For example, the dread of death can become a celebration of a new beginning. In other words, looking at uncertainty and ambiguity relationally gives us the ability to transform our different ways of experiencing the world, each other, and ourselves.

Ambiguity enlivens our humanity. Therefore, the *uncertainty and ambiguity* of communication undercuts domination by undercutting the hegemony of any one meaning. Abdulkarim Soroosh, who is seen by many as Iran's boldest contemporary theologian, contends that certainty and absolutism make for religious dictatorships, such as the one in Iran that now condemns and persecutes him:

> The essence of religion will always be sacred, but its interpretation by fallible human beings is not sacred—and therefore can be criticized, modified, refined, and redefined. What single person can say what God meant? Any fixed version would effectively smother religion. It would block the rich exploration of the sacred texts. Interpretations are also influenced by the age you live in, by the conditions and mores of the era, and by other branches of that knowledge. So there's no single, inflexible, or absolute interpretation of Islam for all time. (Wright, 1999, pp. 46-47)

Instability and creativity are the order of the world. We are constantly seeking new and richer experiences. It is a matter of languages having the ability to ebb and flow so as to allow us to grasp the world and each other deeply and fully. According to Ellul (1994), "Language never belongs to the order of evident things. It is a continuous movement between hiding and revealing. It makes of the play in human relationships something even more fine and complex that it would be without language. Language exists only for, in, and by virtue of this relationship" (pp. 120-121). Ebonics reveals glimpses of this emergent relation. It is deeply relational. It is playful and joyful. It rejects rigid rules and complex structures. It stresses flow by celebrating spontaneity and creativity. It accents contexts over symbols. It affirms life by fostering relationships rather than structures. In addition, research consistently reveals that black communication is highly animated, lively, and forceful (Kochman, 1990). It is seen as being laden with spiritual energy. Blacks show much higher levels of immediacy—communication that enhances closeness—than whites (e.g., Neuliep, 1995). Neuliep contends that blacks use language to establish and sustain community. Gudykunst and Hammer (1988) found that blacks develop and maintain deeper friendships than whites.

Jean-Jacques Rousseau (1986) articulates an interesting theory about language differences that helps explain the differences between

Standard English and Ebonics. He argues that geography explains a lot of the differences between Western and non-Western languages. According to Rousseau (1986):

> Indeed, men of the North are not without passions, but theirs are passions of another kind. In warm climates the passions are voluptuous, related to love and softness. Nature does so much for those who live there, that there is almost nothing left for them to do. As long as an Asian has women and rest, he is content. But in the North, where people consume a great deal and the soil is barren, men, subject to so many needs, are easily irritated; everything that happens around them worries them: since they have a hard time subsisting, the poorer they are, the more they cling to the little they have; to get close to them, to threaten their lives. That is what accounts for their irascible temperament, so quick to lash out furiously at everything that offends them. Their most natural utterings therefore are those of anger and threats, and they are invariably accompanied by strong articulations which make them harsh and noisy. (p. 274)

Rousseau posits that the origin of language is musical. He believes that warm climates make for languages that are lively, resonant, eloquent, and accentuated. Such languages are full of life, warmth, and rhythm. Such languages also thrive upon the spoken rather than written word. On the other hand, the languages of cold climates are rigidly structured. Consequently, "Our languages are better written than spoken, and it is more pleasant to read us than it is to listen to us" (p. 275). The need to prevail in the cold climates distorts the musical tendency of language by suppressing the social dimension of language for the task dimension. The result is the rise of reason and the end of passion. Relationships grow through passion. It is passion that oils and binds and fuels our relationships. Passion is the energy of life.

The differences between languages can also be explained by the fact that certain languages stress coercion and others persuasion. Among peoples who stress persuasion, language must be eloquent and exuberant. It must appeal to passion rather than to reason. It must tap our deepest emotion. Coercion, however, needs no such language. Institutions will do. We merely need to learn how to threaten and punish. In this way, institutions aptly reflect the move away from persuasion to coercion. We claim that the rise of reason is a mark of progress. It shows us realizing a deeper understanding of the world through the development of superior techniques. In reality, however, what is really happening is the rise of coercion. It is coercion rather than reason that explains the progress of Western civilization. The rise of reason can be seen in the fact that Western civilization thrives on the ambition to control the world and human beings. No other peoples have spent comparable resources and energy to have the world and other human beings succumb to the forces of coercion. No other peoples have expressed such a hostility to the world.

I am by no means calling for the end of reason, but rather calling attention to the rise of reason through the suppression of passion. Ideally, languages should allow for the easy expression of both reason and passion. The point I am trying to make is that different relations to the world make for different relations to our languages and that such differences have real consequences.

PRIMITIVE PEOPLES AND PRIMITIVE LANGUAGES

> I will submit that one of the reasons that it [Ebonics] is a problem, if you will—a controversy—is that you cannot divorce language from its speakers. And if you have a people who have been disenfranchised, are neglected, are rejected, it is very difficult for the society at large to elevate their language. And, thus, when you start to try to make a case with legitimizing Ebonics . . . you, in effect, are talking about legitimizing a group of people. You're talking about bringing them to a status comparable to society at large. And that's always a difficult proposition.
> Orlando Taylor, Dean, Graduate School of Arts and Sciences, Howard University

> I'm incensed [about the resolution] . . . the very idea that African American language is a separate language can be very threatening, because it can encourage young men and women not to learn standard English.
> Maya Angelou, Poet

It is popularly assumed that language reflects social evolution. We speak casually about primitive languages and prelinguistic peoples. It is even popularly assumed within the scholarly community that language evolved out of the need to control our supposed striving for strife and aggression. We look at languages as a reflection of progress, reflecting the civility of a community. Conversely, peoples who supposedly lack a standardized language or mastery of one are seen as backward and uncivilized. It is no doubt for this reason that the reaction of the black community was the most visceral. The school board, by granting legitimacy to Ebonics, was seen as officially tying the black community to what is commonly believed to be a primitive language, reinforcing the belief that blacks are primitive. The Oakland school board was seen to be suggesting that blacks lack the cognitive skills to master what is commonly seen as a superior language, Standard English. In this way, the black community saw the resolution as a threat to social mobility as well as reinforcing stereotypes that many blacks have struggled long to dispel. Sadly, missed from all the commotion is how the onus is on blacks to show themselves worthy of being equal to whites. It is a burden that blacks unfortunately have chosen to bear. The reaction to the resolution shows this plainly.

The belief that language reflects social evolution makes for a tremendous fixation with identifying the attributes of different languages that supposedly reveal points of comparison. This approach supposedly allows us to assess the evolutionary condition of different languages, the origins of different languages and, ultimately, identify which peoples possesses what kinds of languages. In a book titled *The Menace of Multiculturalism*, Alvin Schmidt (1997) argues that English is born of "the unparallel greatest of Western civilization." It is supposedly the language of freedom and liberty. According to Schmidt (1997), "English, like no other language, has been the medium by which the British and their descendants, the Americans, fashioned a culture of freedom and liberty that other societies with different languages have not even come close to equaling" (pp. 122-123). He echoes J. R. Joelson's claim that "the world's greatest articles and documents of human rights and freedom were first written in the English language" (quoted in Schmidt, 1997, p. 123). Schmidt then rhetorically ask, "Without being a linguistic determinist, one is nevertheless moved to ask: Why has no other language inspired such monumental hallmarks of freedom? This question is all the more significant when one considers that these documents did not arise in just one culture or in one century. . . . Obviously, this is not a popular position to take today when more and more people have accepted multiculturalism and its contrary-to-fact propaganda that argues all cultures are equal or of equal value" (p. 123).

Schmidt (1997) contends that the lack of democracy and freedom in Latin America is directly related to the Spanish language being devoid of concepts related to democracy and freedom. Consequently:

> Making the United States a bilingual country with Spanish the second language and status equal to English would rupture the nation's social and political stability, similar to Canada's present state of affairs. It would have disastrous effects on the existing American institutions of liberty and human rights. Along with accepting the Spanish language, the United States would receive huge loads of cultural baggage that would greatly deteriorate American culture. (p. 124)

The point is that language has achieved the ability to make distinctions among human beings, resulting in enormous consequences for different groups of human beings. Yet, this hegemony is purely a social construction. It is an artifact of human beings. It is this hegemony, however, that gives language power.

To believe that language reflects social evolution is to believe at a deeper level that human beings are unequal. The hegemony that language now enjoys is merely an artifact of this bedrock belief. It is all possible that any other social construct can be used to reflect our supposed *inequality*. History reveals the use of many different kinds of markers to reflect our supposed *natural* differences. In believing that certain groups are superior and others less so, based again on which group supposedly possesses the superior language, the explicit suggestion is that certain groups act superior to others. In this way, besides reflecting differences, language also supposedly reveals which groups of human beings have the proclivity to act either primitively or superiorly. In this regard, Ebonics is associated with animality. Universal Grammar, however, releases us from the belief that language reflects social evolution. It equalizes human beings. In doing so, Universal Grammar releases us from the notion that the condition of our language reflects cognitive and moral capacity. It is rather the relation that different groups have with language that reveals whether a set of human beings have the proclivity to act either functionally or dysfunctionally.

DIFFERENT CULTURES, DIFFERENT PERCEPTIONS, DIFFERENT EXPECTATIONS

If Ebonics is not a language, then how could we, the Ebonic-speaking community, have understood one another all this time?
Shanee Gibbs, Oakland Technical School

Sooner or later, we must come to terms with a difficult fact. We say we value a multicultural society. Yet there is still a tendency to attack the various colorful and expressive, but non-standard, forms of speech that are at the very heart of cultural identity.
The American Gazette

Behind the Oakland controversy is the belief that a written tradition is superior to an oral one. This belief works in tandem with the others that I have already discussed to maintain the secular hegemony that fosters human separation. It has also made for a hegemony of the written word. As with any other kind of hegemony, that of the written tradition reflects a changing relation to the world—one from cooperation to domination. Its evolution reflects and coincides with our ambition to control the world, to strip away all of its ambiguity and mystery. It also reflects a changing relation to one another—one that is ultimately less tolerant of diversity. Under the label of progress, the hegemony of the written word has evolved. We have surmised that this hegemony is vital to progress—that is, that our meanings must be closed to continuous reinterpretation. The evolution of this hegemony shows a strenuous moving away from ambiguity, reflecting our decreasing capacity to deal with the ambiguity of the world. It also shows the beginnings of us using the past to strenuously control and limit the present.

Oral traditions have been maligned in order to justify and rationalize our fear of separation. The corollary—always—is that one group of people is by nature superior to other groups. In this case, peoples of a written tradition are assumed to be superior to peoples of an oral tradition. Of course, black peoples are traditionally associated with the latter. Consequently, such peoples are commonly seen as uncivilized and uncultured. Yet, the fact is that oral traditions possess many virtues that reveal a lot about human potentiality.

Walter Ong (1967, 1981, 1982) makes many noteworthy observations about oral traditions. Ong contends that the focus on sound makes oral traditions uniquely rich. Human consciousness is interiorized. Only sound pierces and fills up the interiority of human beings. In oral traditions, the world is experienced from inside the body. The world and others are pulled within the body. This makes for a deep experiencing of the world and human beings, as the energy and passion of life remains in the body. It accounts for why oral traditions are highly sexual, sensual, and spiritual. It also helps explain why the dominant religious teachings of the world stress an oral rather than a written experiencing of God, such as preaching and hearing the Word of God. Ong (1982) posits that oral traditions put human beings at the center of the cosmos:

> In a primary oral culture, where the word has its existence only in sound, with no reference whatsoever to any visually perceptible text, and no awareness of even the possibility of such a text, the phenomenology of sound enters deeply into human beings' feel for existence, as processed by the spoken word. For the way in which the world is experienced is always momentous in psychic life. The centering action of sound (the field of sound is not spread out before me but is all around me) affects man's sense of the cosmos. For oral cultures, the cosmos is an ongoing event with man at its center. Man is the *umbilicus mundi*, the navel of the world. (p. 73)

Oral traditions view communication as action. It is about ways of experiencing the world and each other. As Ong (1982) observes, "Our complacency in thinking of words as signs is due to the tendency, perhaps incipient in oral cultures but clearly in chirographic cultures and far more marked in typographic and electronic cultures, to reduce all sensation and indeed all human experience to visual analogies" (p. 76). In oral traditions, words have power. Communication animates the world. Oral traditions are also quantum. We find a constant reinterpretation and elaboration of understandings and experiences of the world, as no set codifications exist to hold them constant. We also often find no ethos that stresses the *capturing* of meanings. This is what makes story-telling such a compelling form of communication. No story allows for any one meaning—a meaning that subordinates all others. What also evolves is a celebration of fiction. Besides story-telling, the oral tradition is rich in poetry and parables. Fiction allows us to transcend the present. It enlivens meaning creation by releasing us from the contours and parameters of our existing reality. Fiction allows us to speak a deeper truth. Oral traditions also foster ambiguity and uncertainty. Such traditions exercise our existential and spiritual striving for meaning creation by constantly demanding of us new and different meanings. We find an organic proclivity for diversity, as no meaning is ever so fixed as to shut out the possibility of other meanings.

Oral traditions foster community. About the uniting tendency of such traditions, Ong (1982) explains: "Primary orality fosters personality structures that in certain ways are more communal and externalized, and less introspective than those common among literates. Oral communication unites people in groups. Writing and reading are solitary activities that throw the psychic back on itself" (p. 69). This uniting is encouraged in many ways. Proximity is vital to the survivability of oral traditions. The close kind of proximity that is required works against—but by no means ends—the evolution of deadly conflict. Consequently, oral traditions tend to possess a vast array of discursive, performative, and communicative practices to diffuse deadly conflict. Ong (1981) and Garner (1994) point to such practices within black cultures, such as verbal play. The collective bearing of community also contributes to the building of community. The lack of a written record *forces* oral peoples to collectively bear the memory of the community. This collective bearing deepens the bonds of community, as the identity of each person lives within the collective memory that the community bears. Oral traditions also bind people through the weaving and reweaving of narratives, story-telling, and poetry. Yet each telling and retelling changes the meanings that attend to each story, poem, and narrative. Thus, what binds the people together is the constant telling and retelling.

LANGUAGE AND DIVERSITY

When a student walks into a classroom and starts splitting verbs and busting infinitives and dangling participles, whether he's black or white, whether she's black or white—or any other color, it's bad English, it ought to be corrected. But to suggest that black kids are the only ones who do that is wrong.

Travis Smiley, Host, Black Entertainment Television (BET)

I can't believe that we are talking about Ebonics as if it really is a condition other than ignorance. If I was an English teacher, I would be up in arms that someone told me I had to translate slang so I could teach somebody English.

Maya Angelou, Poet

Our dominant view of language shows a consciousness that accepts distrust, selfishness, suspicion, fear, and aggression as natural attributes of human relations. We have no qualms believing that human beings possess a propensity for social devolution. We also have no qualms equating our humanity with that of rodents and chimpanzees. It is all of this, however, that is contributing and maintaining the hegemony of the secular. Our distrust and suspicion about our humanity gives us no footing to contest this hegemony. Our apparent amoral, aexistential, and aspiritual nature gives us no moral ground to contest the status quo. Our secular view of our humanity binds us to ways of being laden with selfishness, distrust, fear, and suspicion. Universal Grammar, however, undermines the legitimacy of this secular hegemony. It positions us differently toward the world and each other.

Universal Grammar also gives tremendous weight to any definition of liberation that delegitimizes hierarchy and coercion. Actually, Universal Grammar seems to suggest—and rather compellingly—that human beings are meant for liberation. It is only human beings who, through communication, have the ability to bring meaning to bear upon the world, and, only through Universal Grammar, the ability to give our world endless expressions. In this way, Universal Grammar affirms our distinct relation to the world. It reflects our moral, existential, and spiritual capacity. In telling us something about our being and our capacity, Universal Grammar also tells us something about the nature of the world.

The belief that our languages reflect significant differences is drawn from the worldview that tells us that race, ethnicity, gender, and other such differences explain the origin of hierarchy. We can expect to be told eventually that the size of our earlobes also reflects significant differences that explain why persons with big earlobes tend to be elites of power and wealth. Scholars would spend tremendous resources doing all kinds of research and publish endless books and articles quarreling over the validity of this new claim—about exactly how significant is this construct. Commentators will posit that the matter is still undecided and further research is required, and *The Wall Street Journal* will contest any claim that seeks to discredit the theory of earlobes. The fact is that the status quo must exercise the politics and ethics of separation. New arguments must be constantly peddled or others reinvented—such as IQ—to justify the implications of a politics and ethics of separation. Obviously, the elites of wealth and power are still getting away with this practice. The Oakland controversy reveals that most of us have yet to understand that the origins of slavery and apartheid have nothing to do with race, just as much as the problems that confront the Oakland children have nothing to do with language. Race, gender, ethnicity, and sexual orientation are merely constructs created to justify discrimination and hierarchy. Regardless of how well blacks command Standard English, a mechanism will always be found to justify separation. Slavery, apartheid, and the Oakland controversy all have origins in human separation.

Yet what language is doing is making for a superior hegemony, superior ways of legitimizing the status quo. The Oakland controversy shows the ascendency of language over race, class, and ethnicity. Language allows us to detect, discuss, and act in a discriminatory manner with regard to race, class, and ethnicity without ever having to mention such notions, thereby exposing our prejudices. Rosina Lippi-Green (1997), author of a compelling book about the politics that underlie Standard English, *English With An Accent: Language, Ideology, and Discrimination in the United States*, writes:

> Accent serves as the first point of gatekeeping because we are forbidden by law and social custom, and perhaps by a prevailing sense of what is morally and ethnically right, from using race, ethnicity, homeland or economics more directly. We have no such compunctions about language, however. Thus, accent becomes a litmus test for exclusion, an excuse to turn away, to refuse to recognize the other. (p. 64)

Language gives blacks the illusion that the status quo is finally getting beyond race. It also recruits blacks to help sustain the separation ethos that is vital to preserving the status quo. Language also sustains deep assumptions and beliefs of our humanity that the status quo thrives upon, such as the belief that hierarchy thwarts our supposed proclivity for social devolution and chaos. Lippi-Green (1997) argues that Standard English is premised on numerous myths that are used to legitimize the status quo; such as that language plurality undermines national unity, that different kinds of Englishes are *really* substandard dialects, that Standard English is standardized, and that Standard English is geographically, racially, socially, and politically neutral. She writes convincingly about the ideology of standardization and how educational, political, and media institutions engender this ideology. She defines ideology in the following way: "The promotion of the needs and interests of a dominant group or class at the expense of marginalized groups, by means of disinformation and misrepresentation of those non-dominant groups" (p. 64). According to Lippi-Green (1997):

> The myth of standard language persists because it is carefully tended and propagated. Individuals acting for a larger social group take it upon themselves to control and limit spoken language variation, the most basic and fundamental of human socialization tools. The term *standard* itself does much to promote this idea: we speak of one standard and in opposition, non-standard, or substandard. This is the core of an ideology of standardization which enpowers certain individuals and institutions to make these decisions. (p. 59, italics in original)

Lippi-Green (1997) is also concerned with how minority groups become complicit in promoting an ideology that works against themselves. She sees this being accomplished through rewards, such as the promise of social mobility, and through the constant devaluation of non-standard languages, which makes ultimately for a denigration and rejection of self, race, and identity. The Oakland controversy reflects this kind of complicity. She also discusses research that shows that members of dominant groups tend to put an unfair burden upon nonstandard language users to carry the majority of the responsibility in the communication act. Like race and gender, now language is used to justify our unwillingness to push the bounds of our humanity. We are again spared from risking life. Recognition of the unfair arrangement subtly forces the nonstandard-language user to surrender the nonstandard language for fear of frustrating the person who usually holds access to the promised rewards. In the end, however, such practices by the standard-language user thwart differences by preventing persons from developing ways of being that allow for the articulation of differences. Coercion and punishment are reinforced as civil ways of dealing with differences.

REDUCTIONISM, HOLISM, AND COMMUNICATION

Reductionism leads to a violent way of understanding the world. It forcefully deconstitutes complex relations until truth is supposedly exposed. It strips away the complexity that constitutes life and puts no premium on the complexity that constitutes our humanness. Reductionism also fosters the belief that the origin of language can be found through stripping away the complexity that constitutes human interaction. It divorces language from communication. Most of all, reductionism divorces us from each other and from the world. The origins and purposes of language are assumed to reside within us rather than between us or between us and the world. The academy thus tends to look to our genes and neurobiological structures to understand and explain the origins of language and communication.

We pay no attention to what happens when human beings actually use language or what happens between peoples through language use. Reductionism reduces communication to data, information. Focus is on symbols, codes, and signals. Meaning, context, and relationships are rarely discussed. Focus is on language use and language competency—that is, our command and manipulation of symbols and media. Rarely is any attention paid to our ability to construct meaning, or to the kind of meanings that we construct, or to the discursive and material practices that give rise to certain meanings and suppress others. Language and information are both now conflated with communication. Reductionism masks the ethics and politics of human interaction by reducing communication to symbols, codes, and signals. In deconstituting communication, reductionism deconstitutes our humanness and relationality. It masks the fact that human beings are constituted through meaning, through relationships, through each other, through our relationship to the world. When communication is reduced to information, the effects are perilous.

Information makes for an ethics and politics of transmission. Focus is on manipulating and transmitting our messages. We stress the command of *good* Standard English and *solid* communication *skills*. Rarely is any focus put on the discursive and material practices that help construct our messages, much less to the deep ideological structures that underlie our messages. Information depoliticizes communication. We find no interrogation of how our messages sustain the status quo—that is, no relation is assumed between our messages and the status quo. Hierarchy emerges as purely an artifact of nature rather than an artifact of human beings.

It is interesting to ask why Western civilization has chosen reductionism over holism. What has convinced us that stripping away the world represents a superior way of understanding the world? Reductionism is an artifact of separation. It perpetuates separation. Separation helps us to understand that reductionism is about distrust, suspicion, and anxiety. It represents a certain relation to the world, rather than merely a way of understanding the world. What needs to concern us, however, is the *kind* of truths that reductionism posits about the world and the consequences of such truths. Interestingly, such matters are rarely addressed. We look at truth as truth. We cast ourselves as truth seekers. We claim to go wherever the truth is, report whatever the truth is. It is supposedly the task of philosophers, medical ethicists, and theologians to deal with the implications of the truths of the world. We, as scientists and scholars, simply find and present the truth objectively. This popular view is interesting from the standpoint that our epistemology and truths are assumed to be apolitical and arelational, devoid of biases, prejudices, perspectives, and worldviews. Our epistemology and truths are already from the beginning cleansed and disconnected from contexts and relationships. Reductionism is already present. Our epistemology is supposedly devoid of ethics and politics. The effect of this, obviously, is an unwillingness to scrutinize our truths. We unquestionably accept whatever the scholarly community—especially the physical and life (*sic*) sciences—posit as truth. Any person who even hints of questioning the march of science is accused of mysticism. The *truth* is off limits. Consequently, all that is negotiable are the implications of our truths. This situation serves the status quo well. The status quo gains when interrogation is undermined. Reductionism will always foster separation and separation will always foster a politics and ethics that thwart liberation. In *Sister Outsider*, Audre Lorde put this well: "The master's tools will never dismantle the master's house." What needs to concern us is how to end reductionism so as to help end the ethics and politics of separation.

Communication reveals that holism offers an ethics and politics of union. Communication elevates the reality that our humanness is forged through each other and it binds us to each other. Communication also elevates our relationalness, our proclivity and need for relationships. We are the only beings who develop relations with the cosmos and all of the other life forms that occupy the world. No other being has even remotely shown the ability or tendency to establish such relations. Intertwined with this ability is the potential to end the world as we know it. We are the only beings who have this potential. Whether human beings will eventually do so is dependent on whether union or separation prevails. Further, all of our relationships are organically entwined. Conversely, our relationalness shows us uniquely equipped to help with the completion of the world. We do have the ability to establish relations with the world that complement the forces of union.

Communication reveals that our relations to each are entwined with the condition of the world. Besides politicizing human interaction, communication brings an ethics and politics to human interaction. It describes and prescribes human interaction. Only discursive, communicative, and performative practices that complement union are moral. In this way, communication gives love a moral anchor. It also gives a moral anchor to compassion. Most of all, communication delegitimizes hierarchy and domination, whereas separation disintegrates our relationalness. The end of communication results in community being reduced to networks, friendships to contacts, neighborhoods to suburbs, and peoples to markets. We are atomized. Individualism emerges and selfishness and self-centeredness appears. Theoretical and political schemes to justify such a turn soon arise followed by apathy. Organizing becomes difficult, as no collective interest is assumed. The result is a further undermining of any effort to end the status quo.

Separation comes with many temptations. It requires less of us to simply seek our own selfish interest. It requires the risking of less life. The payoffs also seem to be faster and surer. We are unwilling to wait for the rewards of compassion, trust, and love to mature. We want our payoffs and profits now. Separation also comes with less ambiguity and certainty.

The problem is that no intensity is being derived from our relationships. Our relationships are without passion and joy. Our language moves with no rhythm and our ways of being with neither funk nor soul. It is all classical and mechanical. We have resigned ourselves to merely exist—moving our messages back and forth, and increasingly playing out our intensity rushes in the virtual world. Any fix suffices. It is separation that robs our relationships of passion. Intensity resides within our relationships and represents the fullness of life. It resides in our unselfishness and our willingness to give generously of our selves. It is about the capacity of our relationships to allow for the full expression of passion. Obviously the relation that allows for the most passion is one that is laden with affirmation, compassion, and love. Ebonics bears out this reality. Scholars have consistently commented about the highly animated nature of black communication. It is physical, gestural, and, yes, loud. It is fundamentally relational. It is much less textual than Standard English, as so much of the communication is relational and nonverbal. The reason for the different ratio is passion. Words can convey only so much passion. Knowing this limitation, the nonverbal/relational element of black communication is rich and liquid. It soaks in passion. The expectation among blacks is that meaning belongs to relationships. Whereas Ebonics is about relationships, Standard English is about words. Whereas Ebonics is about communication, Standard English is about information. Whereas Ebonics grooves, Standard English marches. Ebonics releases blacks from any fear of bending and twisting syntax and words. Instinctively, blacks know that the goal is communication, as only communication sustains life. Meaning is properly placed within relationships rather than within words. Ultimately, what matters most is the quality of our relationships rather than the consistency of our codes.

Black communication is shaped by historical forces. The institutional discrimination and persecution U.S. blacks have faced is nearly unparalleled. Blacks have confronted the fullest expression of separation. It was all meant to destroy life—to destroy the will of blacks to resist the separation of slavery. But life being life, blacks had to resist. Blacks had to develop mechanisms to sustain life. No oppression goes unchallenged. The forces of oppression will always be met by the forces of liberation, the reason being that life is a relational phenomenon. Life thrives when relationships blossom. Ebonics is born of blacks resisting dehumanization and death. It is an artifact of liberation. This is why Ebonics complements union rather than separation. Its deep relational ethos is no accident. It is also why Ebonics is fundamentally about communication rather than language. When death and separation are confronted, what is required is communication—modes of being that allow us to grasp life. This is also why affirmation is the dominant ethos of black communication. It is communication rather than information that sustains life. Consequently, linguists are correct: Ebonics has no distinct origin in African languages. On the other hand, linguists miss a key point: Ebonics is about communication rather than language.

Ebonics was forged purely out of the suffering and persecution that blacks faced in the United States. To reject Ebonics is to reject the suffering and persecution blacks have historically faced. It is to reject blacks' survival. Ebonics represents the triumphing of blacks over the forces of oppression and separation. To now contend that Ebonics would thwart social mobility and access for blacks assumes that the forces of oppression are now nonexistent and, moreover, that the status quo offers the platform to liberation. But the status quo offers no such platform. Racism is only an artifact of oppression. Standard English may give blacks access and social mobility but never liberation. Liberation represents union and union represents the negation of everything that Standard English represents. All oppressed peoples have an Ebonics. Ebonics is the language of liberation. Liberation requires communication. All of the peoples of the world need Ebonics. Ebonics belongs to the world. It reflects the questing of human beings to end the forces of oppression. It also represents the affirmation of the past, present, and future. Ebonics shows human beings affirming life.

The Oakland controversy compellingly show many blacks holding to a narrow conception of liberation. It also shows that liberation has been coopted. That blacks were embarrassed about Ebonics shows the legacy of over of 350 years of slavery and apartheid. It seems that for many blacks, liberation is purely about social mobility and access. Unfortunately, many blacks seem to have settled for this cheap understanding of liberation. The fact that blacks nearly unanimously abused the school board show that a new politics and ethics of liberation needs to be forged. Of course, women, homosexuals, and other historically marginalized and disenfranchised people also give currency to this cheap understanding of liberation. But this understanding of liberation poses no threat to the status quo. Inclusion of blacks, women, and others poses no destabilizing threat to our dominant consciousness of the world. In fact, the status quo seems to be striving through inclusion. In the end, separation perpetuates separation. We have to get beyond the politics and ethics of separation. We need new tools. We need a politics and ethics of union rather than separation, an epistemology of holism rather than reductionism, and ways of being that accent communication rather than information. It is a matter of ending the reification of differences rather than diversity. It is, after all, only through union that diversity blossoms. It is also a matter of realizing that the reification of our differences originated in a consciousness of separation. It is also a matter of realizing that our relationships with each have real implications on the condition of the world. Regardless of our race, gender, sexual orientation, and so forth, all of our relationships have to move towards union. All of this is necessary to end domination and hierarchy. Liberation requires much of all of us. We can only end discrimination by ending separation.

We have successfully promoted a shallow and cheap definition of liberation. We believe that human beings have no existential or spiritual capacity for liberation. We look at liberation as something that has to be configured by us. We have successfully cultivated the notion that human beings have no existential and spiritual dimensions. We are descendants of apes and chimpanzees—artifacts of language and competition. We supposedly need hierarchy to suppress and control our violent animal nature. Institutions are supposedly hallmarks of progress and social evolution. Stephen Jay Gould even posits that human beings are a freak accident of evolution. Any definition of liberation premised on union rejects such notions. It is assumed that human beings do have an existential, spiritual, and moral capacity. We do have a moral responsibility to the world. Liberation affirms life. It sustains and fosters the evolution of the world through union. Union with each other represents union with the world, and only through union is the world spared destruction. I have been trying much less to beat down Gould and company than to affirm our capacity for a deeper understanding of liberation. Any theory of liberation that makes no kind of existential, spiritual assumption poses no threat to the status quo. We are given no new vista to look at what being human means.

SUMMARY AND CONCLUSION

Universal Grammar reflects a world of creativity, spontaneity, and diversity. Such features are entwined with the forging of deep and meaningful human relations. Our becoming is related to the becoming of the world. Only human beings possess the capacity to bring meaning to bear upon the world and the capacity to develop deep and meaningful relations. All of which means that our relation to *the spiritual potentiality of the world* is through communion—that is, through union. According to Samuel Hugo Bergman (1991):

> Spirituality is fundamentally a reciprocal relationship. Man's spirit is in its essence a receiving spirit dwelling in a relationship to a giving spirit. . . . The essence of language assumes a reciprocal relationship between people, and it also creates that reciprocity. . . . Language was given, instilled in us from above. The origin of language is in God. Language is transcendental, supernatural, a fact of spiritual rather than natural life. The natural physical-organic life of a person could not find its way to logos [language]; logos finds its way to our physical life and awakens it to the life of the spirit.
> In other words, language is the revelation of God to man. . . . Whoever wishes to explore the essence of language . . . must necessarily believe in God. (pp. 156-157)

Our redemption is dependent on our commitment to ways of being that engender the full blossoming of all of existential and spiritual strivings. This demands, among other things, a new relation to our languages. We need human relations that accent being and becoming. Also, emergent understandings of the world are forcing us to look at the world anew. Such observations reveal an existential and spiritual world. What is also emerging is an understanding that this world is about meaning. The objective is to develop a dialogical relation to the world. This is also what Bohm's *rheomode* is all about. Dialogical communication moves with the consciousness of the world. Only human beings have the capacity to reach new levels of being and consciousness. Thus, to claim that no real distinctions exist between human beings and animals is to posit a different conception of what being human means and a different set of relations with the world and to each other.

We turn our attention next to dominant discourses about diversity occurring within the United States. We will find that a narrow understanding of diversity pervades such discourses. Diversity is commonly defined as biological, racial, sexual, and cultural differences. Our ambition is show how this narrow understanding of diversity makes for all kinds of political and theoretical shortcomings. This narrow understanding of diversity makes ultimately for a politics and ethics of separation. The end result is a belief that the possibility of a real and meaningful understanding of diversity is beyond us. Obviously, I reject this popular belief.

4

Diversity
as Life

What makes standard English standard is a matter of social attitudes and the political power of those who speak the standard dialect. . . . Because standard English speakers control education, commerce, government, and other powerful institutions, the standard dialect is firmly associated with public life.

    Carolyn Temple Adger, Center for Applied Linguistics

The Ebonics controversy is, finally and most importantly, a fight not only apparently about language, but in fact really about language—that is, language as an instrument of influence and social control. . . . I think this will turn out to be the major political issue of the pre-millennium: the determination of who controls language, makes meaning, makes the words that can be used for public discourse, establishes the modality of that public discourse, and determines as a result who and what can and should be listened to and taken seriously. Language may be no more than exhalations of air, but whoever controls language has political control—power.

    Robin Lakoff, Professor of Linguistics, University of California, Berkeley

I am strongly opposed to bilingual education. I believe it divides the country. . . . There are already enough divisions between blacks and whites.

    Peter King, R-New York

Oakland [School Board] . . . strokes the fires of racial misunderstandings.

    Rachel Jones, *Newsweek*

Ebonics is absurd. This is a political correctness that simply has gone out of control.

    Sen. Lauch Faircloth, R-North Carolina

Multiculturalism of the strident sort that the Oakland board has espoused, is no favor to American subcultures. In the short, it may enliven everyone's appreciation of the variety of American styles, but in the long run it can only turn that variety into mainstream mush. . . . Subcultures flourish when they are part of life, not part of the curriculum.

    Louis Menand, *New Yorker*

Would it [Black English], and its survival, make a good subject for a Ph.D. dissertation? Undoubtedly. Can its recognition help toward its abolition? That must be the hope.

    Christopher Hitchens, *Vanity Fair*

[Ebonics] direct workers and youths away from any struggle against the source of social and cultural deprivation, the profit system itself. The myth of Ebonics fuels racism and racial division, while pitting one section of the working class against another for increasingly scarce resources.

    World Socialist Network

This is multiculturalism gone a little haywire.

    William Bennett, Education Secretary (Ronald Reagan
    Administration)

This issue doesn't break down on conservative or liberal lines. In fact, Bob Novak and I tonight are in rare agreement—it must be a full moon—thinking that teaching Ebonics is a dumb idea. . . . [I]f I were an African-American parent in Oakland, I'd be suing the school board for making my kid a second class citizen.

    Bill Press, Host, CNN Crossfire

The nationwide roar of laughter over Ebonics is a very good sign. . . .
[A] big reason for all the chuckling over Ebonics is the decreasing
public tolerance for the politically correct notions lurking in the shad-
ows of this debate—identity politics, victimization and self-esteem
theory. Identity politics means a constant attempt to stress cultural
separateness, so to claim a separate language . . . fits right in.
John Leo, *U.S. News & World Report*

The ruling by the Oakland School District was fodder for opponents
of multiculturalism. The ruling supposedly transgressed the
bounds of cultural civility. It showcased the excesses of multiculturalism. "The whole thing [multiculturalism], this is to say (minimal-
ly)," Marcus Klein (1997) laments, "has gone too far, has got out of hand,
has become a mischief" (p. 75). Interestingly, however, and amply evidenced by the above quotations and many others too numerous to print,
both traditional opponents and proponents of multiculturalism vocifer-
ously argued that the resolution was wrong. Both sides also dealt with
the school board abusively and harshly. In my view, the consensus
reveals no fundamental disagreement between the groups. It seems that
disagreements between both sides have been overblown.

The unison in reaction shows aptly that our common understanding of multiculturalism is morally, existentially, and spiritually
bankrupt. It poses no real threat to the status quo. It undermines the
possibility of liberation. It is bereft of any potential to afford new ways
of being. It is a distraction. In what follows I contend that popular discourses about diversity—toleration versus assimilation—limit our
understanding of diversity through a hegemony of secular assumptions.
I posit that both discourses—regardless of the various versions and permutations—lack any kind of firm theoretical ground. The result is that
both sets of discourses reflect paradoxes, confusions, theoretical shortcomings, and other theoretical mishaps that undercut any understanding of diversity as a potentially existential and spiritual phenomenon
that bespeaks an existential and spiritual world. Further, both discourses
give us a distorted understanding of diversity. Diversity is reduced to
differences, such as race, ethnicity, sexual orientation, and so forth. Such
differences must supposedly be managed for the good of all. We will
find that both assimilation and toleration discourses focus on differences
rather than diversity.

I contend that our deep distrust and suspicion of our humanity
makes for a deep distrust and suspicion of diversity. Both sets of discourses reflect this fear and distrust. Diversity is rarely cast as something
moral, existential, and spiritual. Finally, both sets of discourses reify a
deep fear of diversity. Although assimilation and toleration are commonly seen as representing conflicting positions and different politics,

nothing about the differences is significant. It is really about degrees of distrust of diversity. Diversity needs to be redefined as an artifact of union. In this way, race, gender, ethnicity, and other such social markers are merely preconditions to diversity. Linking union with diversity transforms our understanding of diversity.

CRITICISMS AND COMPLAINTS

What is it that makes for such anger and divisiveness? It cannot be the learning aspect because most educators accept the principle that you have to take students, no matter what background they come from, or where they are, accept what they bring and build on that to push them forward.

    Jerrie Scott, Director of the Office of Diversity, University of Memphis

The African-Americans who responded negatively (to the Oakland proposal) responded out of embarrassment and out of shame. They could not see any value in recognizing that the language of our ancestors was indeed a language. I don't know any other people on the face of the earth who are embarrassed about the language of their ancestors.

    Molefi Kete Asante, Chairman, African American Studies Department, Temple University

Opponents of multiculturalism are often strident about the supposed threats that multiculturalism poses; they say that it undermines evolution, progress, and unity. Proponents of multiculturalism are commonly seen as troublemakers deserving of contempt and scorn for deliberately threatening the stability of the good society. Cal Thomas (1998), a nationally syndicated columnist, writes, "The diversity proselytizers seek to divide, not unite. . . . Their goal is to tear down, not build up. . . . Taken to the extreme, America might come to resemble Bosnia, Northern Ireland or the Middle East. Only in unity do we stand" (p. A11). Opponents contend that what began as a benevolent effort to correct for the neglect of different peoples and cultures has now taken on a new mission—courtesy upstart academics—bent on destroying the status quo by deifying differences, attacking the legitimacy and superiority of Western traditions and institutions, seeking the end of capitalism, rejecting objective truths, and making other kinds of mischief, such as the supposedly stupid ruling by the Oakland school board. In an essay titled *Tenured Radicals: A Postscript*, Roger Kimball (1991) posits:

> Implicit in the politicizing mandate of multiculturalism is an attack
> on the idea that despite our many differences, we hold in common
> an intellectual, artistic, and moral legacy, descending largely from
> the Greeks and the Bible, supplemented and modified over centuries
> by innumerable contributions from diverse hands and peoples. It is
> this legacy that has given us our science, our political institutions,
> and the monuments of artistic and cultural achievement that define
> us as a civilization. Indeed, it is this legacy, in so far as we live up to
> it, that preserves us from chaos and barbarism. And it is precisely
> this legacy that the multiculturalist wishes to dispense with. (p. 6)

Frederick Turner (1996) argues that multiculturalism is born of academics who are from relatively uneducated and uncultured backgrounds. He contends that this group got control of the university only because the supposed *cognitive elites*—whom he deems the rightful and traditional occupants—went off to seek lucrative careers in law, business, and industry. Proponents of multiculturalism, on the other hand, supposedly shunned the rigors of such careers because of the lack of the cognitive gifts vital for success. He no doubt assumes that capitalism makes for a natural hierarchy based on cognitive differences. About the new occupants of the university, Turner says something that warrants lengthy quotation:

> Their [proponents of multiculturalism] encounter with the grandeur,
> complexity, and challenge of the great works of civilization was
> shattering and humiliating, and they did not have the moral or cul-
> tural resources of a family tradition that might have made comfort-
> able and normal a submission to those authorities, and voluntary
> apprenticeship to their guidance. The shame of personal and intel-
> lectual inadequacy was overwhelming. The only response in many
> cases was to seek to undermine and delegitimize those achievements
> by any means possible—by deconstructing them, revealing or dis-
> torting the biases of their authors, by preferring more simple-mind-
> ed texts or ideas from lesser cultural traditions that were easier to
> master, by eliminating them from the curriculum on the grounds of
> including other traditions, and by changing the subject to politics in
> the classroom, the neighborhood, the media, the courts, and city
> hall. (pp. 89-90)

The vulgar nature of this comment is simply stunning. Rather than being robust and vibrant, Turner's argument is cruel and vengeful. Its vulgar nature reflects how much multiculturalism is seen as a threat to the status quo. The level of visceral aggression begs the question of how Turner can claim that proponents of multiculturalism are the real threats to disunity and tribalism. Unfortunately, however, Turner's argument is typical of the opposition to multiculturalism, making again the visceral reaction against the school board ruling understandable, though still uncivil. In *The Menace of Multiculturalism*, Alvin Schmidt (1997) contends that multiculturalism thrives on grand fabrications and malicious distortions. It is supposedly bent on eradicating our "nation's morality, laws, and ethics . . . [and has] an intense hatred of anything that reflects biblical values" (p. 7). It also supposedly aims to destroy U.S. society by pushing a Marxist ideology, promoting homosexuality, rejecting *objective* truths, and replacing Christian morality with pagan values. Like Turner, Schmidt views proponents of multiculturalism as spoiled academics who are "alienated from its [U.S.] capitalistic, Eurocentric values, a culture that has given its people—including those who despise it—more prosperity, creature comforts, freedom rights, and opportunity than any other culture in the world, past or present. Having lavishly benefitted from the abundant fruits of this culture . . . they evidently see no challenges left for them" (p. 17). He believes that ultimately multiculturalism threatens to destroy the *soul* of U.S. society. Supposedly, U.S. society has thrived by obeying God's moral law and by being morally virtuous.

Diane Ravitch (1990 contends that, "At its most basic, our common culture is a civic culture, shaped by our Constitution, our commitment to democratic values, and our historical experience as a nation. In addition, our very heterogeneity sets us apart from most nations" (p. A44). Ravitch believes that proponents of multiculturalism threaten our *common culture* by deifying differences, promoting ethnocentrism, and making no appeal to our common humanity. Dinesh D'Souza (1995) defines multiculturalism as a political movement that rejects Western cultural superiority. He also accuses proponents of multiculturalism of flirting with fragmentation and disunity by blaming Western civilization for all the sins of the world. Richard Bernstein (1994), author of *Dictatorship of Virtue*, also warns of disunity and chaos. He believes that multiculturalism "is a code word for political ambition, a yearning for more power, combined with a genuine, earnest, zealous, self-righteous craving for social improvement" (p. 7). For Dennis O'Keefe, proponents of multiculturalism represent a new-found guilt-ridden perversion for the opulent success of Western civilization, a search by old complainants of the status quo who seek both a new constituency and politics through gender, race, sexual orientation, and ethnicity, and historical and factual trickery. In an essay titled "Multiculturalism and Cultural Literacy," O'Keefe (1994) puts the matter the following way:

> Today the Wayward Elite, as I have named the new clerisy, has largely abandoned its outright espousal of full-scale socialism in

favor of new obsessions with race and gender. All societies seem predicated on some element of self-destruction, some sense that the gods or fates are angry. In the past, religious observance served to channel and control these deep-seated inclinations. Our societies increasingly lack such mechanisms for homeostatic management of anxiety. And where there is both less belief in other-worldly directed worship and more to be grateful for materially, so there is more to be anxious about, and a greater inclination to seek some villains. A society that has largely normalized economic luxury permits its intellectuals a growing self-indulgence. (p. 69)

Multiculturalism is seen as tampering with the superior mechanisms, such as capitalism, that have evolved, thanks to Western civilization, to check our supposed proclivity for social devolution and chaos. O'Keefe (1994) argues that capitalism is responsible for the unsurpassed progress of Western civilization. He believes that competition makes for a vital hierarchy, "Yet the underlying logic of any preemptive attempt to disrupt the meritocratic hierarchies of economic and cultural evolution must ipso facto end up as a form of anti-capitalism" (p. 77). Indeed, most opponents of multiculturalism posit that capitalism is the crowning achievement of Western civilization.

O'Keefe believes that the supposed egalitarian ethos of multiculturalism poses a threat to the supposed progress that competition engenders and to the natural ordering calculus (hierarchy) that thwarts social devolution and chaos. He labels multiculturalism a socialist conceit. It is a popular accusation among opponents. Lewis Feuer (1991) puts the matter bluntly:

> To the extent that a free marketplace exists in the international system, it is American culture and the American language that are accepted as closest to the world's common culture. From Moscow to Beijing, from Johannesburg to Tokyo, it is the example of American institutions that is, consciously and unconsciously, re-shaping the world. Common people, idealistic youths, industrial and artistic communities, and scientists all look to America for the design of progress and the maintenance of order and freedom. They are choosing the world culture of the future, which is essentially American. Those who, in a gesture of secession from American civilization, advocate multiculturalism on American campuses are the latest example of a malady that periodically seems to affect American academic intellectuals. The phenomena of degenerative evolution, as Darwin indicated, still remain to be fully understood. (p. 22)

Feuer posits that proponents of multiculturalism are apologists for the world's cognitively inferior and primitive peoples. He writes, "If multiculturalists succeed in acquiring control of the curriculum, and if they then institute a kind of force-conditioning of students with the literatures and ideological apologia for backward peoples, the consequence for the universities will be quite other than they foresee" (p. 22). His contempt for the new occupants of the university no doubt equals that of Turner.

Feuer assumes that Western civilization is the hallmark of modernization. This kind of rhetorical ploy epitomizes the most pernicious kind of hegemony. It allows Feuer and other prominent opponents of multiculturalism to view any other kind of civilization as backward. But as Samuel Huntington (1996a) points out:

> Modern societies have much in common, but they do not necessarily merge into homogeneity. The argument that they do rests on the assumption that modern society must approximate a single type, the Western type; that modern civilization is Western civilization. This, however, is a false identification. Virtually, all scholars of civilization agree that Western civilization emerged in the eight and ninth centuries and developed its distinctive characteristics in the centuries that followed. It did not begin to modernize until the eighteenth century. The West, in short, was Western long before it was modern. (p. 30)

Huntington posits that U.S. hegemony is actually declining as powerful currents of indigenization have the world moving towards non-Western definitions of modernization. He also argues that Western political and cultural chauvinism runs contrary to Western values and principles. He writes, "The belief that non-Western peoples should adopt Western values, institutions, and culture is, if taken seriously, immoral in its implications" (p. 41). On the other hand, Huntington has deep and real fears. He believes that our focus must be on maintaining the unity of the West against non-Western states bent on making mischief. This demands, among other things, controlling immigration, ensuring assimilation of non-Western peoples into Western culture, and preserving Western culture.

Huntington wrongly reports that English is no longer becoming the universal language of the world. Braj Kachru (1999), widely acknowledged as the leading authority on the proliferation of languages, compellingly argues that this view is contrary to fact. He argues that popular misconceptions about the universality of English is based on many faulty conceptions. He points, for example, to the fact that non-native users of English now outnumber native users. He argues that the world is now witnessing the rise of World Englishes—peoples throughout the world colonizing English rather than being colonized by English. About this phenomenon, Kachru (1999) writes:

> It is a shift, then, from the Judeo-Christian and Western identities of the English language toward its African, Asian, and African-American visions. In these multiple identities of the language the pluralism of world Englishes—the *madhyama*, the medium—is shared by us, all of us, as members of the world Englishes community. The *mantras*, the messages and discourses, represent multiple identities and contexts and visions. The *mantras* are diverse, cross-cultural, and represent a wide range of conventions. It is precisely in this sense that the medium has indeed gained international diffusion; it has broken the traditional boundaries associated with the language. (p. 15)

Huntington also assumes that modernization represents progress. In this way, traditional civilizations, by being less modern, are seen as less evolved and sophisticated. However, tying progress with modernization legitimizes common understandings of modernization. The status quo gains moral cover and it evades rigorous moral interrogation. Moreover, linking progress with modernization sustains a narrow understanding of progress. According to Huntington, "Modernization involves industrialization; urbanization; increasing levels of literacy, education, wealth, and social mobilization; and more complex and diverse occupational structures" (p. 29). He defines modernization institutionally. Within this definition, cultures and peoples who stress cooperation, harmony with the world and each other, altruism, spirituality, are assumed to be less modern.

Huntington perpetuates a hegemony of modernization. This hegemony delegitimizes other understandings of progress, especially those that conflict directly with our own. I am referring specifically to noninstitutionally premised definitions. Finally, linking modernization with progress distorts our understanding of history. Huntington assumes that the telos of history is modernization. We supposedly strive to develop complex and grand institutions. History, however, evidences progress. It shows human beings opposing the forces of oppression.

Much of what Huntington describes as modernization is really progress. It is progress that pushes against racism, sexism, fascism, and so forth. It is progress that tumbles dictatorial regimes. It is progress that is now pushing against modernization. Progress assumes that disequilibrium is the order of the world. In assuming that modernization is the telos of history, and by defining modernization institutionally, Huntington assumes that modernization represents our conquering of our supposed proclivity for evil and chaos. He obviously believes that the West has found a superior way of doing so. Consequently, Huntington believes that the preservation of Western traditions and institutions are vital to our continued progress. He also sees the strengthening of such traditions and institutions as vital to fend off the threats that other civilizations increasingly pose to ours. He writes:

> Maintaining the unity of the West . . . is essential to slowing the decline of Western influence in world affairs. Western peoples have far more in common with each other than they have with Asian, Middle Eastern, or African peoples. The leaders of Western countries have institutionalized patterns of trust and cooperation among themselves that, with rare exceptions, they do not have with the leaders of other societies. United, the West will remain a formidable presence on the international scene; divided, it will be prey to the efforts of non-Western states to exploit its internal differences by offering short-term gains to some Western countries at the price of long-term losses for all Western countries. The peoples of the West, in Benjamin Franklin's phrase, must stand together, or most assuredly they will hang apart. (p. 44)

Multiculturalism no doubt threatens the stability of Western traditions and institutions. In fact, Huntington (1996b) believes that multiculturalism poses a grave threat to the unity and posterity of the West. He contends that multiculturalists reject the existence of a common U.S. culture, engender disunity, and deny the rich cultural heritage of the West. Accordingly, multiculturalism needs to be stopped:

> Rejection of the Creed and of Western civilization means the end of the United States of America as we have known it. It also means effectively the end of Western civilization. If the United States is de-Westernized, the West is reduced to Europe and a few lightly populated overseas European settler countries. Without the United States the West becomes a minuscule and declining part of the world's population on a small and inconsequential peninsular at the extremity of the Eurasian land mass. . . . The futures of the United States and of the West depend upon Americans reaffirming their commitment to Western civilization. Domestically, this means rejecting the divisive siren calls of multiculturalism. (pp. 306-307)

Thus, assimilation needs to be strenuously stressed and immigration needs to be restrictively controlled. Huntington has created a moral and political context that legitimizes coercion and domination. Our survival is supposedly dependent on our ability to suppress any movement that threatens the stability and hegemony of Western traditions and institutions. Obviously, within this context, the ruling by the Oakland school board poses such a threat. On the other hand, Huntington has apparently forgotten that history's most destructive wars—World Wars I and II—

occurred between Western states. Moreover, such wars occurred between modern states.

Assuming that modernization represents progress makes for a deficient conceptual model. It exaggerates differences, heightens our fear of each other, engenders divisions, legitimizes domination, and blocks scrutiny of the status quo. It creates bogeymen. It also has the tendency to oversimplify what being human means by reducing the goal of life to one of survival. It distorts the study of history. To suggest that history represents our aspiration to conquer our evil proclivity assumes that human beings have no other business with the world. We are released of any obligation to look beyond the cultures that supposedly damn us to deadly conflict with each other. We focus on the differences that cultures reflect. Our analyses rarely mention the universals that cultures reflect. The result of downplaying and masking our complexity is the legitimation of a theoretical, political, and moral framework that fosters disunity rather than unity.

OBJECTIVITY AND SUBJECTIVITY

It is completely outrageous yet so totally predictable that the school board's action regarding teaching ebonics is winning praises from the PC liberal/left.

It is racist to suggest, as does the board's action, that African-American students are incapable of learning Standard English, which is the language of commerce, the workplace, government and U.S. society in general.

The real goal of those backing this move is multiculturalism, as opposed to the melting pot society which is what made this nation so successful.

If the U.S. is to remain a leading economic and social force as we enter the 21st century, we must not allow the PC crowd to have its way in imposing multiculturalism on the nation.

Jack D. Bernal, San Francisco

Many opponents of multiculturalism look at Western civilization as the highest manifestation of human evolution. In The *Disuniting of America*, Arthur Schlesinger (1992) explicitly makes this claim. He writes:

Whatever the particular crimes of Europe, that continent is also the source—the *unique* source—of those liberating ideas of individual liberty, political democracy, the rule of law, human rights, and cultural freedom that constitute our most precious legacy and to which most of the world today aspires. These are *European* ideas, not Asian, not African, nor Middle Eastern ideas, except by adoption. (p. 127; italics in original)

Proponents of multiculturalism are accused of denying this supposed objective fact by believing that cultures are beyond objective assessment. Dinesh D'Souza (1995) writes mockingly, "At its deepest level, the intellectual premise of multiculturalism is cultural relativism. In this context, relativism means that all cultures are basically equal. No culture can be said to be better or worse than any other. Cultures are just different, and we must learn to cherish their differences. All cultures are equally entitled to respect" (p. 18). In short, proponents are accused of looking at objectivity as merely a discursive artifact.

Arguably, many prominent proponents of multiculturalism do look at objectivity as a discursive illusion. This view evolves from an emerging perspective that views all of our being and that of the world as merely discursive creations. It is supposedly this discursivity that blocks the possibility of objective standards. For example, Furbank (1997) writes, "What would it mean, even in theory, for a value to be measured? It would mean, if anything, measuring it against some other value, and this would lead to an infinite regression. . . . No meaning can be attached to the idea of measuring (i.e., evaluating) a culture by its own standard of measurement; for a measuring rod, it needs hardly be said, cannot be measured by itself. . . . [T]hough one may try to understand and empathize with a culture not one's own, one must not presume to judge it" (pp. 88-89). Daniel Farber and Suzanna Sherry (1997), authors of *Beyond All Reason*, contend that this emergent discursive thrust—by persons they label *radical multiculturalists*—represents a direct assault on the Enlightenment foundations of our democracy, threatens disunity and chaos, engenders elitism, and cultivates anti-Semitism. They posit:

> Jews have been especially committed to Enlightenment beliefs, and thus have been instrumental in secularizing and universalizing American culture. . . . It is a reciprocal relationship; the Enlightenment focus on intellect and away from pedigree, on achievement rather than biography, on universal rather than local standards of merit, helped open doors that had previously been closed to Jews. To attack that meritocracy necessarily implies that Jewish success is ill-served. Viewing merit as being arbitrary or worse deprives successful minority groups—like Jews and Asians— of any way to defend their attainments. (p. 71)

One of the most prominent proponents of this emergent discursive view, and thus usually on the receiving end of the criticisms of opponents of multiculturalism, even that of Farber and Sherry, is Stanley Fish. Fish (1997) makes a distinction between what he labels *boutique* multiculturalism and *strong* multiculturalism. Boutique multiculturalism is about representation and expression of different lifestyles and cultures. Focus is on respecting differences to the extent that such differences allow for the representation and expression of other cultures and lifestyles. Violation of this understanding is reason for sanction. Boutique multiculturalism stresses restraint of belief and subordination to the common good. The chastising of the Oakland school board by traditional proponents of multiculturalism is boutique multiculturalism. The school board supposedly violated the bounds of decency that all cultures must respect, threatening the common good.

Strong multiculturalism on the other hand looks at such restraint as a violation of differences. It stresses constructive engagement so as to protect differences between cultures and lifestyles that are fundamental and conflicting. Although Fish believes that strong multiculturalism is superior, he also believes that the lack of any objective framework—as regards engagement—and the perils of toleration make any kind of coherent multiculturalism impossible:

> It may at first seem counterintuitive, but given the alternative modes of multiculturalism—boutique multiculturalism, which honors diversity only in its most superficial aspects because its deeper loyalty is to a universal potential for rational choice; strong multiculturalism, which honors diversity in general but cannot honor a particular instance of diversity insofar as it refuses (as it always will) to be generous in its turn; and really strong multiculturalism, which goes to the wall with a particular instance of diversity and is therefore not multiculturalism at all—no one could possibly be a multiculturalist in any interesting and coherent sense. (p. 384)

Fish concludes that any meaningful multiculturalism cannot be either affirmed or rejected. Understandably, the relativist assumption that undergirds Fish's argument makes for no other kind of conclusion. He, moreover, believes that no predetermined solution with overarching principles can fix our multiculturalism problems, as multiculturalism is too undefinable:

> What it means is that the solutions to particular problems will be found by regarding each situation-of-crisis as an opportunity for improvisation. . . . Any solution devised in this manner is likely to be temporary—that is what ad hoc means—and when a set of problems outstripped its efficacy, it will be time to improvise again. It follows that definitions of multiculturalism will be beside the point,

> for multiculturalism will not be one thing, but many things, and the many things it will be will weigh differently in different sectors of society. (p. 386)

Yet Fish's formulation is really no solution at all. No moral objective ground exists to arbitrate tensions between conflicting groups that are probably convinced that might always makes right. Still, Fish believes that this is the best that could be had. Any one who rejects this conclusion becomes vulnerable to being either a *boutique* or *strong* multiculturalist, or a blatant and vulgar nativist seeking the colonization (homogenizing) of peoples with a certain worldview. As Donald Pease (1997) observes, "Fish makes clear his interest in restricting his argument with liberalism to the dimensions of its failure to realize on its own grounds a discourse—a set of attitudes and agents able to effect them—of multiculturalism. As a consequence, he puts himself under no obligation to engage an understanding of multiculturalism that is not grounded in the assumptions of liberalism" (p. 401).

The way that Fish construes multiculturalism—that is, dichotomously—releases him of any obligation to entertain other understandings of multiculturalism. Fish constructs a reality in which only two kinds of multiculturalism can possibly exist. Interestingly, Fish is constantly criticizing others for employing such kinds of rhetorical ploys for selfish and devious ends. Anyway, what Fish ultimately gives us is nihilism. By tossing out the possibility of progress, which he does by rejecting the possibility of any meaningful framework and dismissing any serious consideration of any kind of an objective moral calculus, all that is left is nihilism. What is also left is coercion, which Fish (1989) openly concedes. (In *On Matters of Liberation* I discussed this matter at length.)

Fish legitimizes nihilism by viewing progress as a myth. Supposedly, no truth transcends discursivity. The possibility of different peoples peacefully coexisting is also a myth, as any secular framework that is agreed upon to this end undermines the formation of deep beliefs. Toleration asks peoples to accept beliefs, values, and practices that they find morally wrong. Such peoples, according to Fish, are obligated to resist and abolish, say, homosexuality, for doing anything less constitutes a lack of conviction and even sin. As a result of this tension, Fish posits, toleration eventually (and always) gives way and vicious conflict ensues between conflicting groups. He sees no end to conflict, war, and tribalism. The result is always nihilism.

The temporary and ad hoc approach that Fish espouses is actually about constructing relations that both sides view as having the capacity for mutual retribution and hopefully—yes—the possibility of mutual destruction. If a side manages to beat this arrangement, and this is always the goal, for all the reasons just discussed, then the other side faces the threat of annihilation, and justly so. Accordingly, all relations between peoples with different worldviews are, and must be, laden with deception, making for only tenuous relations and temporary solutions. This formulation, however, violates the bounds of theory. Fish shows no theoretical understanding of the consequences of deception. Deception fosters dysfunctional conflict. It blocks the open expression of conflict. It blocks disequilibrium. In doing so, deception blocks the catalyst that is vital for growth, development, and transformation. Deception undercuts life by blocking the evolution of trust, empathy, diversity, compassion, and all that springs from the development of deep and meaningful human relations. Such relations undercut the tribalism that Fish believes is ultimately unavoidable by engendering everything that negates tribalism. Tribalism is an artifact of distrust and deception rather than trust and transparency. Fish, moreover, assumes that cultures are homogenous constants, without any underlying currents of dissent and conflict that can potentially threaten the status quo. All systems, however, have points of disequilibrium—that is, points of dissent, conflict, diversity, and tension that are the origins of transformation. This is an axiom of system theory. Such points act as catalysts for growth and development by challenging the system to deal with conflict and diversity. Without this constant exercising, the system becomes complacent and moves toward death and devolution. Disequilibrium is the catalyst of life. It is integral to human and collective development, for it gives us the opportunity to look at the world anew. In disturbing our cognitive, sensual, and spiritual stability, disequilibrium catalyzes transformation. In this way, points of disequilibrium organically destabilize the stability of our discursive and material practices, making for the evolution of new practices that represent new ways of being. Differences and disequilibrium are entwined.

Fish also believes that the consciousness of the world passively tolerates deification. The reality is that systems with rigid structures lack the flexibility vital for growth and development. The demise of such systems is certain, as history aptly shows. Flexibility reflects diversity and permeability. It also reflects growth and development. Fish compounds the matter by adhering firmly to the popular belief that tribalism is about *differences*. Rigid structures foster homogeneity by blocking the open expression of conflict that makes for diversity. Such structures limit what meanings are brought to bear on the world. Homogeneity is an artifact of conflict suppression; its hegemony represents devolution and death. The consciousness of this world disallows the longevity and stability of cultures with rigid structures and practices. In assuming that human beings are purely discursive creations, thereby amoral, aexistential, and aspiritual, Fish assumes that human beings have no relation to the consciousness that brings harmony to the world. He rules out any possibility for growth, development, and transformation by dismissing the possibility that human beings have the capacity to transcend cultural differences that foster tribal strife. But as John Bowen points out, the common view of tribal group conflicts rests on many mistaken assumptions. Bowen (1996) compellingly debunks the assumptions that tribal identities are ancient and unchanging; that these identities motivate people to persecute and kill; and that tribal diversity itself inevitably leads to violence. He argues, and correctly so, that what now passes for tribalism is an artifact of political mischief for selfish material gain by select groups (usually elites). Tribal strife is about selfishness and fear rather than ethnicity and race: "It is fear and hate generated from the top, and not ethnic differences, that finally push people to commit acts of violence" (p. 9).

Fish also sees no relation between diversity and cognitive complexity. Cognitive complexity represents our threshold for ambiguity. It is a nurtured capacity. Our level of cognitive complexity determines whether diversity is dealt with empathically and functionally or coercively and dysfunctionally. High levels of cognitive complexity make for the transcending of cultural locations, even beyond the location of strong multiculturalism. Persons with such levels have cognitive structures that are permeable and flexible as a result of continuously adapting and readapting to the ambiguity of the world. Such persons have an aversion to structures that undercut permeability and flexibility—the kinds of structures that undercut our ability to deal with diversity functionally and empathically. In this way, persons with a high threshold for ambiguity thwart the stridency and militancy that foster deadly tribal conflict.

Anything that remotely points to something existential and spiritual about human beings—such as peoples of different backgrounds, religions, politics, and so forth transcending differences and together constructing new religions, new races, and so forth—undermines Fish's argument. As Stephen Whitfield (1996) astutely observes: "The sensibility that has replaced cultural pluralism tends to subvert the belief that particularity can be transcended, tends to discredit the faith in individual talent and in independence of mind" (p. 445). Fish has no choice but to dismiss the possibility of a theoretically coherent multiculturalism. In disbelieving that human beings have moral, existential, and spiritual strivings, Fish's argument reeks with fear, suspicion, and distrust, the constituting elements of all dysfunctionality. Fish's theory gives us no means to disrupt the status quo. It is reactionary, as moral relativism contributes nothing to ending the status quo. In addition, Fish's cultural relativism gives us no calculus to get beyond our fixation with homogeneity. It is bereft of any compelling reason as to why diversity is life affirming. We are given no compelling existential or spiritual argument for diversity. In this way, Fish's cultural relativism merely reinforces the hegemony of the secular. He can tell us nothing meaningful about love, compassion, trust, kindness, and other universals of human beings. That this kind of argument continues to hold much sway within the scholarly academy is no doubt a reflection of the despair that now pervades so much of the world.

Opponents of multiculturalism have pounced on the equalizing and relativizing of all cultures. Phillip Devine (1996), author of *Human Diversity and The Culture Wars,* accuses proponents of relativism—he too gives Stanley Fish considerable attention—of threatening cacophony and chaos. He contends that relativism undergirds (what he labels) both *strong* and *weak* multiculturalism. He makes easy work of what Fish and company call theory. He argues that an objective (nonsecular) moral calculus is vital to any meaningful politics. He writes: "We need a vision of social life that combines an appeal to abstract right and a conception of a society protective of those unable to defend themselves in the world of politics and the market" (p. 103). Devine believes that human beings have to be reaffirmed as persons rather than merely discursive beings: "The simplest and best response to tribalism is that underneath our differences we are all human beings, and as such we have a common core of rights and duties (and we can aspire to practice a common core of virtues)" (p. 120). In addition: "Our common humanity provides a basis for dialogue among diverse men and women—however unclear the character of that humanity might be, and however difficult such dialogue might appear in practice" (p. 149). Devine believes that only the Western tradition, "with its emphasis on the dignity and uniqueness of each individual, provides the only acceptable resolution of cultural conflict" (p. x). What makes this tradition particularly attractive for Devine is the centrality of a Christian conception of God. He believes that the foregrounding of a Christian conception of God guards against the threat of tribalism. Apparently, Devine has forgotten that brutal wars have long been fought among nations who professed a deep Christian faith. He also seems to have forgotten that Christians—as with any other religious group—who publicly profess a deep faith reject the kinds of restraint that he believes is ultimately necessary for the making of a society tolerant of different peoples and lifestyles. For such Christians, tolerance represents the violation of faith. Consequently, compromising and uncompromising groups will clash. Though Devine admits that his notion of a Christian America has numerous porous spaces, this admission by no means lessens the theoretical and political confusion that attends to this notion. In short, his argument collapses quickly when he articulates his own solution to cultural conflict.

Other opponents of relativism contend that it undercuts cultural comparisons and hinders the possibility of progress by putting certain discursive and nondiscursive practices beyond the bounds of moral scrutiny and condemnation. Dennis O'Keefe (1994) puts the matter this way:

> Certainly the multicultural enthusiasts seem to be pursuing a dangerous path. If they assert very loudly that Western culture is not superior, what are their grounds? Have they objectively weighed our culture and others and found none out in front creatively? Are they claiming to have done the comparisons and found no scale of achievement separating cultures, or are they saying that such comparisons cannot be made? If they claim to have done the work, where is it? . . . .
>
> If what is involved in multiculturalism, however, is simply an a priori conviction that no culture can be better than another, what serious spirit is going to be bound by that? Slavery is no worse than freedom? A culture that outlaws eating people cannot be reckoned morally better than one that does not? A modern political culture that produces Auschwitz or the Gulag is not inferior to the representative democracies? This makes multiculturalism a program for the emancipation of cretins. (p. 72)

Blaine Fowers and Frank Richardson (1996), authors of an essay titled "Why is Multiculturalism Good?," contend:

> If we condemn such practices [e.g., female circumcision] as inhumane and insist that they be stopped on the basis of supporting human dignity and basic human rights, we are clearly imposing our standards of behavior on them. This is indeed a cruel dilemma because it pits two of our deepest ethical principles against each other in a profoundly wrenching manner. Multiculturalism seems to be impaled on both horns of this dilemma, for many cultures' ideas about human rights and dignity are not even remotely similar to ours. (p. 615)

Fowers and Richardson (1996) also contend that multiculturalism undermines moral conviction:

> Multiculturalism's relativism undermines the moral force of any universal argument, especially in light of the particularist roots of these ideals in Euro-American cultures. For how could one defend the principles of cultural equality, tolerance, and respect within a relativistic viewpoint? Whence do these universal principles arise?

How can they be taken as universally valid? Clearly, it is inconsistent to promote a thorough neutrality toward all cultures as prescribed by central, cherished ideals of the Euro-American constellation of cultures. (p. 616)

Other opponents claim that multiculturalism is an artifact of Western civilization. Chilton Williamson (1996), who believes that multiculturalism violates biblical teachings, writes: "An openness to other cultures is probably the deepest source of the multiculturalist impulse in America: an inherited European peculiarity, not an African, Asian, or Latin American one" (p. 137). In other words, only Western civilization supposedly seeks the end of sexism, racism, and other forms of tribalism that other cultures sanction as good and sacred. Thus, according to opponents, the promotion of multiculturalism values violates cultural sovereignty. Fowers and Richardson (1996) posit:

Multiculturalism is often seen as one of the remedies for this violence and hatred. If hostile groups could come to understand one another better and appreciate their differences, they would be less inclined to mutual slaughter. This may or may not be possible, but the recommendation that other cultures adopt our multicultural ideals does not show respect for their self-understanding. This may be the ultimate irony of multiculturalism—the imposition of our ideals of tolerance and respect on other groups who hold ethnocentric or racist views! (p. 615)

In *A Dream Deferred*, Shelby Steele (1998) argues that multiculturalism is born purely of opportunism by both whites and blacks. It gives whites a cheap moral currency. Whites can appear morally virtuous by simply tolerating the victimization woes of blacks. On the other hand, multiculturalism allows blacks to profit from mediocrity and to establish and protect racial "thiefdoms." Steele (1998) writes:

Multiculturalism, like identity and self-esteem, is a contingency trigger because its primary goal is not to illuminate culture but to obligate institutions to open up exclusively black territories and monopolies, and to remove excellence as a barrier in this process. The unique character of black American culture—its many art forms, its religious rituals, its manners and customs—is of very little interest in a multiculturalism that reduces minority cultures to the theme that best triggers white obligation: victimization. (p. 53)

Steele also argues that multiculturalism suppresses the rich cultural variety in the United States and represents an assault on democracy by promoting primitive atavisms. He, however, expresses no concern about the moral credibility of a system that makes for an increasing gap between rich and poor, or the legitimacy of the standards that are used to assess merit. He believes that discrimination is an aberration of U.S. society and has no structural or institutional origins. It is simply a matter of blacks and women being willing to get up and get. He believes that diversity interferes with the integrity of U.S. society and democracy. He writes glowingly about the moral virtues of U.S. democracy. Remarkably, however, Steele blames multiculturalism and liberalism for race causing the conditions "by which moral authority is pursued in the United States." He is no doubt forced to make this absurd claim so as to avoid explaining how U.S. democracy long legitimized slavery and an apartheid system against blacks, women, and many others even after many nations abandoned such practices. How could multiculturalism be blamed for such horrors when even Steele admits that multiculturalism is a 1960s phenomenon? Yet Steele insists on blaming multiculturalism for undermining the principles and practices—such as fairness and merit—upon which U.S. democracy supposedly depends. Peddling such an absurd claim insults the memory of the many peoples who paid dearly for calling upon U.S. legal institutions to exercise such principles for all U.S. citizens. In addition, U.S. society has no deep historical record of fairness or equality of opportunity. Race (and gender and class) has always determined the terms of moral authority. Moreover, according to Steele: "Multiculturalism is the kind of thing that happens when a democracy loses the moral authority to protect the individual citizen as the only inviolate unit of rights" (p. 130). Again, no occasion in U.S. history supports this claim. U.S. history is one of institutional discrimination against all kinds of citizens. Even now, discrimination against homosexuals remains legal and institutional in the United States. Evidently, Steele uses multiculturalism to deflect scrutiny from a system that continues to reek with institutional discrimination, and to suppress any serious look as to why U.S. democracy has always being riddled with such discrimination. His ambition is really to defend the status quo.

No doubt multiculturalism has been deliberately caricatured for malicious purposes so as to avoid any transfer of power to historically disenfranchised and marginalized groups. To call for the respect of all cultures by no means represents an end to critical analysis of different cultures. Mark Nathan writes: "What it [cultural relativism] does mean is that we must look carefully at what other people are doing and try to understand their behavior in context before we judge it. It means that other people may not share our desires or our perceptions. It also means that we have to recognize the arbitrary nature of our own choices and be willing to reexamine them by learning about the choices that other people have made" (quoted in Cohen, 1998, p. B4). Moreover, Anne Phillips (1997) writes: "Multiculturalism does not require an a priori commitment to the equal value of different cultures. It does, however, require us to view our own culture as one among many, and this certainly means rethinking what we might have considered transcultural absolutes as more parochial expressions of a particular culture" (p. 58). Indeed, most proponents of multiculturalism look at it with a view toward members of minority and other disenfranchised groups attaining proportional cultural, social, political, and economical representation. As Gloria Ladson-Billings (1992) posits: "Multiculturalism . . . is about difference—not difference as deficit, not difference as something wrong, but difference as diversity and diversity as a value-added phenomenon" (p. 309).

It is, however, difficult to give proportional representation to cultures and peoples who are seen as primitive and backward. Feuer, obviously, is unequivocal: "The pretense too of an equally valid or perhaps superior African culture tends to collapse when the enthusiast for Central African culture becomes mindful that disease and massacre have been its principal offerings" (p. 21). In sum, no moral ground exists to surrender any ground to other cultures and peoples.

Charles Taylor (1994) argues that proponents of Western civilization mistake hegemony for superiority. He writes: "The peremptory demand for favorable judgments of worth is paradoxically . . . homogenizing. For it implies that we already have the standards to make such judgments. . . . By implicitly invoking our standards to judge all civilizations and cultures, the politics of difference can end up making everyone the same" (p. 71). Proponents of Western civilization are unfazed by this kind of criticism. Proponents of multiculturalism are challenged to explain why peoples throughout the world are (supposedly) adopting Western traditions, and capitalism is rapidly spreading to all corners of the world. On the other hand, proponents of Western civilization remain adamant that proportional representation comes at the cost of undermining a superior culture. In *Closing of The American Mind*, Allan Bloom (1987) puts the matter bluntly:

> Cultural relativism succeeds in destroying the West's universal or intellectually imperialistic claims, leaving it to be just another culture. So there is equality in the republic of cultures. Unfortunately the West is defined by its need for justification of its ways or values, by its need for discovery of nature, by its need for philosophy and science. This is its cultural imperative. Deprived of that, it will collapse. The United States is one of the highest and most extreme achievements of the rational quest for the good life according to nature. What makes its political structure possible is the use of ratio-

> nal principles of natural right to found a people, thus uniting the
> good with one's own. Or, to put it otherwise, the regime established
> here promised untrammeled freedom to reason—not to everything
> indiscriminately, but to reason, the essential freedom that justifies
> the other freedoms, and on the basis of which, and for the sake of
> which, much deviance is also tolerated. (p. 40)

But most proponents of multiculturalism wish to do nothing of the sort. Again, the objective is merely to gain proportional social, cultural, and political representation for minority and other disenfranchised groups. Nothing about this ambition poses any threat to the hegemony of Western civilization. The reaction to the school board resolution shows this conclusively. The fuss is about the unwillingness of the dominant culture to yield any ground at all. In fact, the few proponents of multiculturalism who seek to go beyond this mission are rebuked by traditional proponents. The latter warn about the excesses of different strands of multiculturalism. Amitai Etzioni (1996), a traditional proponent, writes: "By relentlessly classifying and distinguishing between Americans—by stressing diversity but not the elements that bind us— we further diminish our already weak and weakening commonalities: We face the danger of coming apart at the seams" (p. 9).

Through hegemony, opponents of multiculturalism have successfully put the onus on proponents to show the virtues of cultural pluralism and how the cultures of minority and disenfranchised groups are comparatively equal. This puts proponents of multiculturalism in a bind and exposes the structural flaws that underpin popular understandings of multiculturalism. By being unwilling to contest the superiority of Western traditions, proponents are then forced to show that other traditions are comparatively equal, yet doing so undermines the superior status of Western traditions by legitimizing all traditions as equally good. In this regard, means must be found to have representation without tampering with or contesting the superior status of the dominant culture. It is, however, this claim of superiority that proponents of the dominant culture use to discredit multiculturalism by casting other cultures as backward and primitive. According to Chilton Williamson, "The United States is threatened less by a plurality of cultures and of languages than it is by a plurality of *moral* languages" (p. 136). He reinforces this point by quoting Lawrence Auster, author of *The Path to National Suicide*, who writes: "The defining concept of multiculturalism is that our society is a collection of equal cultures, from which it follows that America's dominant Western culture is illegitimate and must be dismantled or dramatically weakened." It seems that only opponents of multiculturalism understand that any kind of equalizing poses a threat to hegemony. The result is a multiculturalism project that is deeply mired in political and theoretical hypocrisy, which makes for the endless fodder that opponents exploit.

The evolution of a narrow and harmless understanding of multiculturalism springs from the fact that the dominant culture is us. To contest the dominant culture is to contest our own ways of being. To discredit the dominant culture is to discredit our own ways of being. To challenge the superiority of the dominant culture is to challenge our own superiority. We obviously wish to do nothing of the sort—that is, upset our own hegemony. Consequently, most of us actually want a narrow definition of diversity and multiculturalism so as to avoid scrutiny of worldviews and ourselves. The Oakland controversy exposed us badly.

Our commitment to cultural pluralism is disingenuous. We are unwilling to surrender anything significant. We have deliberately embraced a shallow definition of multiculturalism so as to sustain our hegemony. Gloria Ladson-Billings (1992) contends that multiculturalism is even good and vital for the making of the good society: "Multiculturalism promises that through diversity we will not allow democracy to fall victim to conformity. It means that our diversity mitigates against homogeneous viewpoints that may lead us to accept totalitarian and oppressive forms of governance. It ensures checks and balances, healthy opposition, and democracy" (p. 309). It is this kind of "bargain deal" that now makes multiculturalism status quo. The bargain deal allows for the easy coopting of diversity. It also makes for a superior form of policing. Persons daring to contest popular definitions of diversity are now set upon by proponents of multiculturalism. Who, after all, is better equipped—with regard to legitimacy—to deal with the school board than the president of the oldest civil rights organization in the country and other elites within the black community? Opponents of multiculturalism have obviously recognized the hypocrisy of proponents, which probably helps explain the meanness that characterizes the criticisms of multiculturalism. Without any firm moral or theoretical ground, proponents of multiculturalism are defenseless against such assaults. Any call for equal representation directly challenges the supposed superiority and hegemony of Western civilization. However, as most proponents of multiculturalism wish to do nothing of the sort, the result is a multiculturalism without any firm moral or theoretical ground.

TRIBALISM AND SYMBOLISM

It goes without saying . . . that language is also a political instrument, means, and proof of power. It is the most vivid and crucial key to identity: It reveals the private identity, and connects one with, or divorces one from, the larger, public, or communal identity.

James Baldwin, Author

Oakland's board members say they are trying to rescue African-American students who are drastically over represented in remedial and special education classes. The sentiment is noble. But the best way to boost student performance is to raise standards and hold students and teachers to them. Anything less holds the risk of educational surrender. That is why civil rights advocates and black intellectuals have condemned Oakland's plan.

The New York Times, Editorial

Last week's unanimous vote by Oakland's school board resurrected the ludicrous idea that a vernacular form of English—in this case, what is called black English or Ebonics—should be recognized as a primary language. . . . But, in the desire to be culturally sensitive, let's not lose sight of one key goal: mastery of standard English. That is the single best route to decent jobs and higher education in this country for students of all backgrounds. Anything that distracts schools and students away from that path is a foolish diversion.

The Seattle Times, Editorial

Our preoccupation with the preservation of cultural practices and symbols also shows the moral and theoretical bankruptcy of popular understandings of multiculturalism. We aggressively seek the elimination of what are seen as derogatory symbols. It is believed that such symbols cause hurt. Unfortunately, much less attention is paid to explicating the origins of the discursive and material practices that make for the construction of such symbols. Symbols, after all, are merely artifacts of being. It is our distrust, fear, and suspicion of our own humanity that requires derogatory symbols to pin on others who are seen as different and supposedly inferior to us. It is we who bring hurt to others. Our validation of domination, subordination, manipulation, and coercion is what makes for racism, sexism, heterosexism, and other sorts of tribalism that our derogatory symbols only reflect. Our unwillingness to take the analysis to a deeper level undercuts any effort to torpedo the hegemony of the dominant culture. The focus on symbols poses no threat to the status quo: It is a distraction. It is, however, a costly and perilous distraction. Without a commitment to a deep analysis, no serious effort can be made to affect the status quo, opening the possibility of new ways of being that accent the existential and spiritual rather than the secular and material. The commitment to forging deep and meaningful human relations—relations laden with spontaneity, diversity, equality, compassion, kindness, and empathy—will remain nonexistent. In my view, this is the real cost of sustaining popular understandings of multiculturalism and diversity.

What is driving much of the criticism against multiculturalism is fear. We fear that multiculturalism will bring disunity and chaos. It is believed, as opponents claim, that proponents of multiculturalism fan the flames of hatred and distrust. Opponents play to the destruction and bestial behavior that is now evident in Sarejevo, Kosovo, Rwanda, Northern Ireland, and other places, and at a deeper level, to our deep distrust and suspicion of our humanity. We have already seen that opponents claim that *only* Western civilization has the superior mechanisms—such as capitalism—to stop social chaos, fragmentation, and barbarism.

We also fear that the different immigrant groups that are increasingly populating our country will vehemently reject the forces of assimilation. Supposedly, this rejection will undercut the homogeneity and unity vital to progress. Opponents of multiculturalism warn ominously that the negation of the hegemony of Standard English and Western civilization will eventually lead to deadly tribal strife. In *The End of Racism*, Dinesh D'Souza (1995) writes:

> Even more than homogenous societies, multiracial societies need a *lingua franca* [common language]. If most Americans spoke English and new immigrants all spoke Spanish, a bilingual compromise would be reached in which natives learned Spanish as a second language and immigrants learned English. But in a society with many different groups and many ancestral languages—Spanish, Hindustani, Urdu, and Tagalog—we risk an American Babel, a breakdown of communication, if everyone does not speak a shared language. For reasons of practicality, this language must be English, which is rapidly becoming the global medium of intercultural communication. (p. 546)

It is this kind of sentiment that is making for emergent legislative efforts to have Standard English recognized as the official language of the United States. The common belief is that homogeneity—by way of assimilation—is necessary for unity. Conversely, heterogeneity or diversity is the antithesis of unity. It is also assumed that assimilation is supposedly necessary to funnel diversity towards unity. This is accomplished by removing those features, such as language, that are obstructing, or potentially obstructing, the assimilation process. Unity supposedly demands the deletion of the most distinguishing features of the different groups.

Yet assimilation never occurs democratically. It is the dominant group that decides and demands—through coercion and punishment—

which features minority groups surrender. The goal is unity through homogeneity. Our fear of diversity reflects our own fear of the ambiguity of the world. No amount of cultural homogeneity can protect us from becoming another Sarajevo or Rwanda. *What is happening with Sarajevo and Rwanda has nothing to do with cultural diversity or the promotion of multiculturalism.* Our destiny resides with our relation to the ambiguity of the world. When ambiguity is dealt with dysfunctionally, dysfunctional ways of being appear, the goal of which is to end all ambiguity. We also find a deep fear of anything that represents ambiguity, such as diversity. It is this fear that causes the tribal hatred and conflict now racking every corner of the world. Consequently, peoples afraid of ambiguity reveal a visceral distrust and suspicion of our humanity. Robert Bork (1996) writes: "Real human beings do not have any unfulfilled capacity for love, or at least a large one; they simply do not regard men as infinitely precious. . . . Any program for society based on such vapors is headed for disaster. . . . Attempts to suppress aggression entirely and to substitute love, being unnatural, will finally erupt in greater aggression" (p. 28). Schmidt (1997) posits: "In light of the Balkan disaster, why do intelligent people still promote multiculturalism? Why do they not see that multiculturalism does not work? It never has, and it never will, for as long as human nature remains what it always has been, multiculturalism will produce more ills than it will cure" (p. 17).

Peoples afraid of ambiguity use the past to control the present. We find a worship of the dead. Rituals, myths, traditions, and other cultural artifacts are used to suppress conflict so as to block any evolution of differences that can potentially affect the status quo. We also find a hegemony of law. Law sustains the past through precedent and tradition. In fact, law is seen as a superior way of dealing with ambiguity. Consequently, peoples afraid of ambiguity are usually staunch proponents of law and order. Law is prescribed for all disputes and conflicts. There are commonalities among peoples who have a staunch proscription for law, peoples who have a fixation with homogeneity and purity, and the oppression of peoples who are perceived to be different. I am referring to the fact that fascism is characterized by a deep law ethos. Ian F. Haney López (1996), author of *White by Law*, persuasively discusses how elites of wealth and power use law to construct races so as to justify discrimination and maintain privileges. He writes:

> Rather than simply shaping social racial identity, however, the operation of law also creates the racial meanings that attach to features in a much more subtle and fundamental way: Laws and legal decisions define which physical and ancestral traits code as Black or White, and so on. Appearances and origins are not White or non-White in any natural or presocial way. Rather, White is a figure of speech, a

social convention read from looks. . . . It is upon this seed of racial physicality that the courts imposed the flesh of normative racial meanings, establishing the social significance of the very racial categories they were themselves constructing. Only after constructing the underlying racial categories could the courts infuse them with legal meanings. The legal system constructs race by elaborating on multiple levels and in various contexts and forms the meaning systems that constitute race. (pp. 16-17)

Homogeneity reflects dysfunctionality. It represents death and devolution. Diversity, on the other hand, challenges the vitality of systems. This is also an axiom of system theory. Diversity forces systems to develop new ways of being. It sustains permeability and flexibility. In possessing a natural striving for life, systems possess a natural proclivity for diversity. That is, without any kind of coercion, systems sustain diversity. On the other hand, homogenous systems lack permeability and flexibility. We find a strident emphasis on order and control through coercion, domination, manipulation, and subordination. We find rigid and complex structures. We find hierarchy. Hierarchy, again, forces the system to suppress the open expression of conflict. Hierarchy disturbs the natural harmony between diversity and homogeneity. System theory entwines unity with diversity. Unity is an artifact of deep and meaningful human relations. Unity is about human relations laden with trust, compassion, and empathy. It is about union. System theory also stresses the complementary nature of opposing forces. Systems need both diversity and homogeneity. If diversity represents creativity and spontaneity, homogeneity represents stability and continuity. Systems need both sets of elements. The goal is always harmony. In this case, harmony represents any relation that allows for evolution and transformation.

As stated before, a deep fear of the ambiguity of the world makes for the evolution of rigid structures so as to end all ambiguity. Such structures, however, lead to devolution and death by undercutting creativity, flexibility, and permeability. Moreover, rigid structures stifle volition by limiting the possibility of new ways of being. Ambiguity exercises our ability to act deliberately and purposely on the world. Volition is the means by which human beings transform and transcend the present. Volition reflects our ability to act purposely and deliberately upon the world. We can do so only within a relational context. Moreover, without volition or even any kind of human striving, morality becomes purely discursive, and reduced to nothing. In *Democracy and Moral Development*, David Norton (1991) puts the matter well:

What is the right thing to do in given moral situations? What is the best life for a human being? For the particular human being one is?

To entertain these questions is worthwhile only on the premise that human beings possess freedom of appropriate kind and measure. If what each of us shall do and become is without alternative, the notion of choice is illusionary, and it is upon the opportunity to choose that the meaningfulness of the above questions depends. That most of us presuppose the reality of choice is evident in the conduct of our lives. We take seriously a host of decisions, ranging from such life-shaping ones as which vocations to pursue, and whether to marry, and whom, to the plethora of lesser choices that fill our days, such as whether to accept a particular social invitation or read a particular book. (p. 1)

The reaction to the Oakland school board shows the workings of the politics and ethics of separation. Inadvertently, the resolution emerged as a threat to the status quo. It was a threat that had to be violently put down. For the school board to have gotten a different reaction, specifically a nonviolent one, our politics and ethics would have had to be different. Still, what is revealing is *how* the resolution emerged as a threat, and why, say, our commitment to circumscribe a race and class of people escapes any kind of comparable wrath.

DIVERSITY AND DEVOLUTION

On theoretical grounds alone it is unlikely that the mastery of curriculum-central linguistic skills like reading and writing would be unrelated to the language that children bring with them to the classroom. And empirically, studies both in Europe and the United States have shown that with other factors held more or less constant, the ways in which schools respond to the vernacular dialects of their pupils can play a major role in the children's chances of success.
   John R. Rickford, Linguist, Department of Linguistics, Stanford University

Opponents of multiculturalism posit a deep suspicion of diversity. Yet, history refutes the belief that homogeneity is vital to unity. We have seen unparallel levels of human destruction within relatively homogenous groups. The ghastly wars of this century among relatively homogenous groups suggests that homogeneity has nothing to do with the making of the good society. However, Peter Brimelow (1995), author of *Alien Nation*, is adamant that unity is dependent on homogeneity. He believes that the fact that disunity and chaos are wracking supposedly relatively homogenous peoples only shows how even the smallest of differences threatens civility and unity. Accordingly, Brimelow argues that only homogeneity and purity can ultimately prevent disunity and chaos. Evidently, within this framework, even gender, sexual orientation, religious persuasion, and height are threats to unity and progress.

Brimelow seems to want a society that is of one religion, one gender, one ethnicity, one race (preferably of Northern European descent), and one level of IQ. He obviously believes that our proclivity for evil is real. He is explicit about this: "I argue that the force that makes human differences an unavoidable, albeit not unmanageable, social reality is also precisely the force that makes individuals sacrifice their lives for their children. Whether this is nasty or profoundly noble is a matter of taste. Probably it is both. Either way, it exists" (p. xvii). Brimelow is concerned about the supposed pollution that diversity brings to supposedly advanced peoples. He tells us about the low cognitive skills of different peoples and how Richard Herrnstein and Charles Murray's (1994) *The Bell Curve* was unfairly received. He challenges us to confront our supposed unwillingness to deal with the *truth* about certain peoples being cognitively superior to others. Yet, the high visibility that Herrnstein and Murray's book received shows that no such unwillingness exists. As Randall Kennedy (1995) observes, the *success* of this book is revealing:

> The ability of Herrnstein-Murray to reach the highest levels of visibility rests not only on the perceived plausibility of black intellectual inferiority. It rests as well on a willingness by the higher-ups in public opinion management to permit the continued sullying of blacks' racial reputation. Two things in particular contribute to this malign toleration. One is the inability of the black community to discipline effectively those who defame or negligently permit the defamation of African Americans. Not withstanding all the loose talk about political correctness, it is still largely true that journalists, scholars, and politicians can (and do) show disrespect or even outright antagonism towards blacks without paying much of a price. A second contributing factor also has to do with the convoluted politics of political correctness. Some arbiters of public opinion clearly felt the need to demonstrate publicly that they are not in thrall to PC oversensitivity. To demonstrate independence they joined the pack of journalists whose attention quickly made The Bell Curve into a profitable news item. (p. 185)

Brimelow is explicitly articulating deeply held beliefs that our society cultivates. Chilton Williamson (1996) even asserts that the Old Testament legitimizes overt and even institutional discrimination:

In fact, nearly all cases involving sanctuary referred to in the Old Testament and recorded in classical and medieval times rested not on Holy Writ but on legal code and custom; moreover, this right of sanctuary normally was observed for a limited period of time only, and granted to malefactors guilty of a type of misbehavior we recognize today as civil disobedience. It is certainly a mistake . . . to assume that a tradition of sanctuary, originating in the Judeo-Christian conscience and inspired by the Holy Spirit, has been shaped and sharpened by the intervening institutions of Western civilization and delivered to us as a hallowed norm. Rather, it was abandoned when it began to obstruct the uniform law that replaced the arbitrary and localized practices with which it was meant to contend. (p. 152)

Williamson is just as vehement as Brimelow about the pending threats that multiculturalism supposedly poses to the United States's social evolution and progress. He also believes that there is an unwillingness to confront harsh truths for fear of violating the normative sentiment nurtured by what he and many opponents of multiculturalism casually refer to as the *liberal establishment*. The result is that multiculturalism is treated as a political rather than moral concern. But as the threats of multiculturalism are now supposedly reaching critical mass, Williamson believes that a moral obligation exists to expose the hypocrisy—"the offensive superficiality"—and point to the *real* truths. He contends, "A man may be morally justified in laying down his life for his friend; but a government that sacrifices the lives of its citizens to the welfare of strangers has no justification, either in law or in religion, for its act . . . [T]he opening of their borders by the nations of the West in the interest of alleviating Third World chaos would only guarantee the spread of chaos globally" (p. 155).

We would expect Brimelow and Williamson to be deeply suspicious of our humanity. It is this belief that makes for the fear of the Other. We have already seen that persons who call for harsh measures to deal with the Other also have a deep distrust and suspicion of human beings. Bork and others show this relation plainly. It is assumed that stopping social devolution demands coercion and hierarchy so as to arrest our proclivity for chaos and social devolution. So, again, what supposedly makes Western civilization superior is the recognition that human beings are evil, and our development of superior schemes to check social devolution. In this way, Bork and company are claiming that what makes for a primitive society is the lack of any recognition of our supposed proclivity for evil and the necessary standards and controls to arrest social devolution. The fact that capitalism is seen as the best mechanism means that any society that has a less developed capitalist system or no such system is primitive.

Byron Roth (1994) argues that Charles Darwin's natural selection theory reveals that the origins of ethnocentrism and group conflict are biological rather than cultural or political. He writes:

> The truth is that the teaching of ethnic and racial hatred is very limited in comparison with teachings admonishing citizens to be tolerant and accepting of differences. If ethnic and racial enmity continues to exist, it suggests that it is all too natural and not that it is taught. Put another way, if group animosity were the result of teaching, then preventing such teaching, or teaching against intolerance, should be eliminated. The fact that hate is such an easily learned lesson and tolerance a difficult one suggests that the propensity for enmity to arise between groups is there to start with. (p. 195)

Roth contends that our unwillingness to deal with the truths of our biological nature undermines our understanding of group conflict and, thus, our ability to limit such conflict. In fact, Roth believes that the validity of popular understandings of group conflict—most of which are environmentally premised—is highly questionable:

> The problem with [the] environmental or nurturists point of view is that it is disconfirmed in too many cases. Perhaps the nurturists have the causation backwards. This is certainly not to deny that many, perhaps all, conflicts involve some real conflict of interest over resources or political claims. But all too often it appears that groups fight with each other not so much because they have a rational conflict of interest, but rather because they are driven to fight with each other and then justify their hostilities, after the fact, with the most readily available rationale. In other words, maybe it is natural (though unfortunate) for people of different genetic makeup to view each other as biological adversaries and to take the existence of real or imagined grievances as the justification for violent confrontation. Perhaps the grievances are merely the occasion for the expression of hostility and are, in and of themselves, relatively unimportant in causing it. (p. 197)

Roth contends that though group conflict is unavoidable, a policy that reduces the saliency of ethnicity and race limits such conflict. He believes that natural selection theory favors a politics of assimilation rather than toleration. Interestingly, however, Roth makes no mention of the increasing saliency of social class groupings, or any suggestion about decreasing the saliency of such groupings. He delimits diversity to ethnicity and race. Yet, most group conflict springs from wealth distribution and the allocation of resources.

The fact is that opponents of multiculturalism can point to no research that shows that dysfunctionality is a result of a proclivity for evil. No research has controlled for neurological, social, and cultural factors. In *On Matters of Liberation* I argued that such factors lead us to question—really doubt—whether this proclivity is even real. I argued that hierarchy actually engenders social devolution by thwarting human and collective development. Dorothy Lee (1987) found that various native groups throughout the world had ways of being that deemphasized coercion, hierarchy, and competition. Yet, such peoples were without the criminality and animality that are ubiquitous to our own society. On the other hand, opponents of multiculturalism look at our high level of criminality and animality as an aberration that has no bearing on the superior ethos of Western civilization. After all, opponents contend, other cultures and peoples have criminal elements, all human beings supposedly possess a proclivity for evil and animality, and, finally, only a small proportion of our population behaves criminally. It is believed that the most punitive forms of punishment will deter criminality and thus make for the good society. Conversely, our high levels of criminality merely reflect our supposed unwillingness to deal punitively with transgressors and deviants. However, absolutely no research shows that punitive measures thwart criminality. Also, compared with other cultures with significantly lesser amounts of criminality, ours is already the most punitive.

TECHNOLOGY AND HOMOGENEITY

We should not devote limited educational funds and resources which could be used to create greater access to computers in our schools, for example—to Ebonics. Our children must be prepared to compete in a world that does not trade in Black English. They must not be placed at further disadvantage in the competition for jobs by being required to learn Ebonics, while children of other ethnic backgrounds are mastering standard English, advanced mathematics and, yes, computers.
Earl Graves, Editor-In-Chief, *Black Enterprise*

The emerging technology explosion potentially promises levels of assimilation that are now mostly unimaginable. In bringing about the end of the *tyranny of geography*, emerging technology also threatens to bring about the end of *differences* through the homogenizing of cognitive schemes. A popular criticism and concern within the academy is that lifestyles and cultures will be homogenized, as this emerging technology will make for a kind of virtual mall that would be equally accessible to all, regardless of geography. This emerging technology acts as a cultivator of consumerism and materialism, displacing lifestyles and cultures that hold to different values. Through the evolution of emerging technology, a capitalism ethos potentially threatens to end lifestyles and worldviews that accent cooperation rather than competition.

It is also likely that emerging technology will give the elites of wealth and power the ability to better monitor the rest of us. This technology affords superior disciplining. We can expect that as long as our distrust of our humanity remains constant that this technology will be used deliberately—presumably for the valid reason of maintaining order and civility—to oppress diversity. However, rather than lifestyles, what I fear most is the homogenizing of different worldviews. The reality is that emerging technology reinscribes the world and our humanity linearly. Growing dependency on this technology by nonlinear peoples represents the most pernicious kind of domination. Of course, nonlinear peoples traditionally have oral traditions. This emerging technology—which is textually based—represents the threat of a new kind of colonialism. Oral peoples risk being textually colonized through this emerging technology.

The popular notion that emergent technology constitutes progress is laden with questionable assumptions. It assumes that progress constitutes our ability to control our environment. It assumes a conflict between us and the world. Our survival is supposedly dependent on our ability to control and harness the forces of nature. This kind of ethos makes for a deep distrust of nature. Technology represents our ambition to control the unwieldy forces of nature that threaten chaos and devolution. Obviously, no existential and spiritual relation is assumed between us and nature. Our redemption is supposedly dependent purely on our ability to control the forces of nature. No God will save us. We have concluded that to win this contest with nature, nature must be stripped of all complexity. In this case, the goal of transparency is vulnerability so as to afford superior domination and manipulation of nature. In seeking the end of complexity, *man,* through technology, seeks to arrest all the mystery and ambiguity that nature possesses. The result is the end of diversity. Leaving uninterrogated the view that technology represents progress sustains assumptions that make for an overly narrow definition of progress.

THE NATURE OF ASSIMILATION

If we look at the people who do not conform to [Standard English] expectations, we notice that they are often the victims of oppression—people of color, the working class, and the poor. What compounds this is that all three groups are usually the same—people of color are often the working class poor. The ideology of [Standard English] is really not the ideology: it is hegemonism rooted in fear that is based on racial, ethnic, cultural, economic class, or gender difference. That in itself is based on naivete, narcissism, and a lack of an ethical sense and critical conception of history. . . .

I am not saying that African Americans should not speak or write in [Standard English]. I am also not saying that mainstream white Americans should not speak Ebonics. What I am saying is that it is a choice, and the choice for African Americans has been very limited historically because we have been told that our experiences do not matter or that they are not relevant, in part, because they are different and therefore inferior. We are again told that we have to melt; we have to accommodate another's sociocultural and historical contexts because ours are not acceptable. That is not acceptable.

Sonja Lanehart, Assistant Professor of English and Linguistics, University of Georgia

A bedrock belief of proponents of assimilation is that homogeneity is vital for the making of the good society. It is a condition for unity. Whatever quarrels exist are about form, definition, and means. The result is endless arguments about Standard English as our official national language, English as a second language (ESL), bilingual education, affirmative action, content of school curriculum, immigration, school prayer, and gay rights. The numerous arguments no doubt give the impression that vigorous discussions are occurring about what multiculturalism means. In reality, however, no such discussions are really occurring. All discussants already hold to the premise that homogeneity is vital for the making of the good society.

Many scholars now openly call for a return to an assimilation program. It is believed that only assimilation can engender the unity that can stop us from becoming a Sarejevo or Rwanda. In *Assimilation American Style*, Peter Salins (1997) argues that assimilation is at the foundation of our supposedly unsurpassed prosperity, social cohesion, and overall superior evolution. He is surprised that many persons—whom he describes as nativists and strident multiculturalists—would even dream of tinkering with a process that has supposedly spared us from disunity and chaos, and made for our greatness. In fact, Salins is appalled. He writes:

How could America's intellectual and political leaders be so shortsighted as to cast away thoughtlessly the paradigm of assimilation that had proved invaluable in unifying the nation for over a century and a half? . . . .

The history of the past thirty years has shown that America's opinion and policy elites made a terrible mistake by turning away from assimilation and negating the assimilation contract. And it has, indeed, been the country's leaders—the media, in education, in government, and in corporate America—who have been specifically responsible. The rank and file of ordinary Americans were never consulted, and if they had been, they would have rejected the abandonment of the assimilation paradigm. But regardless of where the fault lies, if ever there was a time to promote assimilation, it is today. . . . The United States' two-hundred year history of maintaining national unity while accommodating ethnic diversity may be robust enough to withstand a temporary defection from the ethos and practice of assimilation, but it cannot withstand it for long before a host of unhappy consequences is unleashed. (pp. 15-16)

As with other vociferous opponents of multiculturalism, Salins warns ominously of the dangers of cultural and racial disunity and chaos that can result from our abandonment of assimilation:

In the end, though, the greatest danger looming for the United States is interethnic conflict, the scourge of almost all other nations with ethnically diverse populations. Assimilation has been our country's secret weapon in diffusing such conflict before it occurs, and without a strong assimilationist ethos, we leave ourselves open for such misfortune. Assimilation is not really about people of different racial, religious, linguistic, or cultural backgrounds becoming alike; it is about people of different . . . backgrounds believing they are irrevocably part of the same national family. It is this belief that allows them to transcend their narrow ethnic loyalties and that blunts, to the point of insignificance, the spurs of ethnic conflict and discord. (p. 17)

Salins attacks both nativists and multiculturalists. He believes that a modern assimilation project can avoid the pitfalls of both groups and still foster national unity and cultural plurality. This brand of assimilation obviously appeals to peoples who are uncomfortable with nativist stridency, yet, on the other hand, fear the tribalism that multiculturalism supposedly engenders. In this way, Salins' emergent brand of assimilation really promises a kinder and gentler form of multiculturalism.

Salins looks at assimilation as akin to religious conversion. The tenets of the religion that seeks our conversion are: (1) everything that the U.S. Constitution espouses; (2) a commitment to market capitalism; (3) the density and redundancy of institutional life; and (4) a commitment to modernity and progress that permeates all of society. The conversion is to occur through an educational system that demands proficiency in Standard English and has a curriculum with what he describes as objective and neutral scholarship. Salins knows only too well that this demand will meet no firm opposition: "American culture does have a distinctive base, and that base, from the nation's beginning, has been English. . . . Because of its importance, language is the one feature of American culture that is not optional, even under America's flexible rules of assimilation. . . . On this point, social commentators across the spectrum of cultural ideology . . . agree" (p. 86).

The reaction to the school board validates Salins' point. Yet, the brand of assimilation that Salins advocates is really one of submission rather than conversion. It is all about coercion. Our alienation is assured by the negation of any opportunity to alter any of the doctrines of the religion that demand our conversion. It is the Other who must always adjust and conform. It is the Other who must always be subservient and obedient. Salins' dread warnings about disunity and chaos reflect his belief that human beings possess a proclivity for social devolution, fragmentation, and destruction. He misses, however, how his brand of assimilation identically resembles the kind that leads to the tribalism he warns ominously about:

> Every nation has the right to homogenize its own people as long as
> it's done in a democratic and humane way.
>   Slobodan Milosevic, President of Serbia

In no way am I suggesting that Salins harbors fascist views. The point is that assimilation, regardless of the brand, fosters a fear of diversity that is born of a deep fear of human beings. Dictators and tyrants always point to human beings as possessing a proclivity for evil that must be stopped at all costs so as to afford the good society. Accordingly, Salins' brand of assimilation merely represents a kinder and gentler way of checking our supposed destructive ways. But the unity that assimilation promises is no unity at all. Although Salins chastises us for presumably turning away from our assimilation-oriented ways that are supposedly saving us from disunity, our society can make no claim of ever having the unity that only assimilation supposedly engenders. As Salins acknowledges, our supposedly proud assimilation-oriented past never stopped virulent forms of racism and discrimination against blacks and other minority groups. It also never stopped sexism, heterosexism, and other kinds of racism and religious persecution. Discrimination against homosexuals is still legal in the United States. Yet Salins treats our assimilation record with blacks as an aberration. He is confident that blacks will eventually become full-fledged members of the religion. On the other hand, Salins also makes no compelling case that assimilation is sparing us the social chaos of a Kosovo. Rising separatist groups, increasing religious stridency, resegregation of neighborhoods and schools, the suburbinization of racial and social class enclaves, the growing gap between rich and poor, all suggest that assimilation is hardly ending disunity. The reality is that the origins of our discriminatory ways are fundamental to the religion that Salins proclaims is without fault. Equality undermines the status quo. To view all human beings as equal obligates us to give all human beings equal resources and means to excel. A cursory look at the tremendous disparity in school spending between urban and suburban schools reminds us that this obligation is nonexistent. Yet, Salins contends that the proposition of equality is only bridgeable through assimilation. It is a thesis that reality rejects.

The proposition of equality that is embedded in the Constitution was meant to safeguard us from the Other so as to disallow our own subordination and oppression based on the notion that our humanity is unequal. It was never meant to stop our own subordination and oppression of other human beings, specifically blacks and Native Americans. It is for this reason that the framers of the Constitution had no moral urging to end slavery. But what makes the Constitution most appealing is the focus on liberty. Liberty legitimizes modern capitalism. Modern capitalism is even seen as the highest expression of liberty. This explains Salins' commitment to modern capitalism as a goal of assimilation.

Peoples who claim that all persons are unequal and that competition makes for the good society are constantly seeking justifications as to why a few must ultimately get so much and so many must get comparatively much less. It is always about legitimizing discrimination and exploitation. We have never seen a justification for equal distribution of resources. When any justification emerges, discrimination based on that justification quickly follows. Rarely has any justification emerged from the many to justify exploitation of the few. On the other hand, devising supposedly objective means to justify our exploitation of others is a natural reflection of our deep distrust and suspicion of our humanity. Competition demands that opponents harness every opportunity to win, and this demands subordinating others by whatever means necessary.

On the heels of Salins' book is John Miller's (1998) *The Unmaking of Americans: How Multiculturalism Has Undermined the Assimilation Ethic.* His arguments are nearly identical to those of Salins. He also warns that multiculturalism and nativism threaten disunity and chaos, and expresses the need for a strong national identity rooted in Anglo political principles, specifically the U.S. Constitution. The culprits, again, are academics. He sees proponents of multiculturalism—the "Global Village People"—as akin to curators of a national history museum. They are also accused of undercutting the transformative attraction of

Americanization, fracturing U.S. identity, and wanting the United States to look like the United Nations. Miller (1998) writes:

> The constant chatter of derision aimed at the idea of Americanization has had harmful consequences. It has undermined public confidence in the country's ability to assert itself in the vigorous way necessary to make assimilation work. The fallout has included a series of public policies hostile to the Americanization of immigrants. Racial preferences encourage immigrants to think of themselves as members of groups rather than as individuals. Multicultural education does the same thing to students with its nonstop cheerleading of racial and ethnic entitlements. Bilingual education prevents thousands of children, especially Hispanics, from learning the language they will need to know to commit themselves fully to the American way of life. Foreign-language voting ballots are throwing one of the most important institutions of American democracy, the voting booth, into linguistic disarray. (p. 8)

In a facetiously titled book, *We Are All Multiculturalists Now*, Nathan Glazer (1997), about whom Salins writes glowingly, also laments the supposed loss of an assimilation ethos to a multiculturalism ethos. According to Glazer (1997):

> It is multiculturalism in education—so strongly denounced by so many powerful voices in American life, by historians, publicists, labor leaders, intellectuals, the occasion for so many major battles in American education during the nineties, and so much at odds with the course of American culture, society, and education at least up until the 1960s—has, in a word, won. . . . I feel warmly attached to the old America that was acclaimed in school textbooks. Despite all its faults and errors and prejudices and, if you will, crime, it did, after all, bring into its fold over time, though not without political conflict and even Civil War, the people and races it had rejected; it did offer them opportunities; it did correct its errors and faults and to some extent make reparation for the harm its laws and practices imposed. (pp. 4-5)

Glazer contends that multiculturalists are now controlling the content of our education curriculum and this potentially threatens national unity and even civil harmony. About this threat, he writes:

> I do not dismiss fears that a necessary degree of national cohesiveness would be threatened as a result of some kinds of multicultural education. But some of the dominant trends in multicultural education—for example those that emphasize the contribution of various

ethnic groups—should not have this effect, and might well strength-
en national loyalty. If the emphasis moves to oppression, discrimination, grievance, certainly the effects could well undermine national
unity. One would have to see more examples of multiculturalism
curricula, more examples of how they operate concretely in the
schools, before one could make a judgment. (p. 45)

Glazer also articulates many of the arguments that Salins presents. He, too, believes that emergent understandings of assimilation
need to address fears of cultural emasculation; make the educational
system the focal point of assimilation; stress the acquisition of Standard
English; ground the assimilation project in the values and beliefs that
U.S. society holds sacred; protest strident forms of multiculturalism; and
bring blacks into the assimilation project. As regards blacks, however,
Glazer is wary. He even owns up to his own previous underestimation
of the willingness or ability of whites to deal with blacks humanely. It is
this continued derogatory treatment of blacks that fills Glazer with
reservation about the potential of assimilation. Unlike Salins, he is
doubtful that any brand of assimilation can remedy the problem soon:

Only twenty years ago we could still believe that African Americans
would become, in their ways of life, their degree of success, their
connection to society, simply Americans of darker skin. I still believe
that will happen eventually. But our progress in moving toward that
goal, while evident in some respects, shows some serious backslid-
ing, and more than that, a hard institutionalization of differences,
one example of which is multiculturalism in American education. It
is not easy to see how these institutionalized differences will be
overcome soon. (p. 149)

Glazer offers no analysis as to why discrimination against blacks
remains rampant. He believes that the rise of multiculturalism is a result
of the exclusion of blacks from U.S. mainstream society. He warns about
how the language of blacks—and he is sounding this before the Oakland
ruling—is drifting further away from Standard English. Glazer believes
that the making of this distinct language, Ebonics, further harms blacks.
He would no doubt contend that the ruling by the Oakland school board
is only a natural progression of events that is heading us towards disunity and chaos.

Opponents of multiculturalism never mention how the growing
disparity of rich and poor threatens national unity and civil harmony. In
addition, our dominant worldview apparently has no bearing on our
looming disunity, though Glazer and Salins and other opponents of multiculturalism well know—as evidenced by the history of blacks—that

unity has never been realized in the United States. What supposedly also has no bearing on our supposed looming disunity is the distrust of our humanity that is foundational to our worldview. For opponents, only multiculturalists and nativists are to be blamed for undermining unity and civil harmony. Yet despite all the fear cultivated by opponents, Glazer acknowledges that no available proof exists—even after presumably taking over the curriculum—that multiculturalism has brought disunity and disharmony. He and Salins also admit that assimilation has yet to bring the promised national unity. It seems weird, then, to claim that multiculturalism threatens unity and civil harmony when the horrendous treatment of blacks and others demonstrates that this supposed unity and civil harmony has never been achieved. How could multiculturalism be blamed for disunity when no unity ever existed? As multiculturalism is only a recent phenomenon, which Glazer and Salins admit, certainly a better question to ask is why assimilation has never achieved the promised unity. But rather than focus on this matter, opponents of multiculturalism have sought to use multiculturalism as a bogeyman.

The reality is that assimilation has never been forsaken. The fear of our humanity that permeates so much of our being has always led to a fear of differences and of the Other. Nothing about this fear has changed, consequently nothing about our ways of dealing with the Other—as amply shown by the reaction to the school board—has fundamentally changed. As long as our distrust of our humanity remains constant, assimilation will always remain a supposedly valid approach to dealing with differences. We will always be convinced that differences represent disunity and chaos.

The possibility of social disunity and civil disharmony is always real. I fear that persons who even hint of a multiculturalism bias—and remember that nothing is really threatening about popular understandings of multiculturalism—will be blamed for any perceived threat to our unity and stability. Moreover, I fear that the status quo—out of desperation and the frenzy created by the endless ominous warnings of social fragmentation and chaos—will revert to harsher kinds of coercion to foster unity, under the guise of the need to hold our society together. History shows a real possibility of this trend emerging. In fact, the threat of using legislation against the school board and the legislation of Standard English as the national language, among other measures, show that this trend is real. A real possibility exists of such an approach compounding the problem further and thereby exacerbating social disunity and civil disharmony, leading to even harsher kinds of coercion to end differences and a further entrenching of monological ways of being.

There is no doubt that Western civilization reflects progress. It does seek complex moral codes and the development of sophisticated institutions and traditions. On the other hand, I reject the claim that Western traditions and institutions are superior and, as a result, need to be preserved. I reject the assumptions that undergird this popular belief. I also reject the fear on which this belief thrives. Opponents of multiculturalism are telling us that Western civilization is the best that can be had, that it is *man* at *his* best. To reject Western traditions and institutions is supposedly to flirt perilously with chaos and human devolution. Accordingly, the West has to be preserved, has to be heroically defended, and opponents have to be controlled and revolts suppressed. I reject what Western civilization assumes about human beings. I also reject the claim that fascism is an aberration of Western civilization. Fascism reflects the homogeneity that the West *really* desires.

I have argued that Western traditions retard our understanding of diversity by reifying differences. They foster disunity rather than unity. In undermining our understanding of diversity, Western traditions and institutions block our understanding of liberation by enlivening a deep distrust and suspicion of our humanity. Moreover, proponents of Western civilization such as Samuel Huntington engender cultural and moral relativism just as much as opponents like Stanley Fish. Both stress the preservation and protection of cultures; neither recognizes nor appeals to our common humanity. In fact, Western civilization thrives on reifying cultural differences. Moral and cultural relativism gives Western civilization the context to claim its supposed superiority. It encourages a preoccupation with our traditions and institutions rather than with the universals that all human beings possess. Moral and cultural relativism moves the focus away from human beings and toward traditions and institutions. It downplays our common humanity. We are superior because our traditions and institutions are supposedly superior—superiority is measured by our ability to control our supposed proclivity for chaos and devolution.

THE NATURE OF TOLERATION

I think that the coverage of Ebonics shows our uneasiness with our changing culture. Power erodes. The power that was there is gone, the power belongs to everyone. And going after your own kind of language is a power.
Jean Gattywilson, University of Missouri

Language is culture. It is very important that a child's language and a child's culture be recognized and valued.
Noma Anderson, Chairperson, Department of Communications Sciences and Disorders, Howard University

While I am aware that there will always be cultural dialects, and that standard languages themselves are in constant flux, I think there is a great value in establishing a norm. America does not have to become the tower of babble in order for people's unique contributions to be respected and valued.

Armstrong Williams, Washington, Afro-American

The school board in Oakland, California, blundered badly last week when it declared that black slang is a distinct language that warrants a place of respect in the classroom. . . . But by labeling them linguistic foreigners in their own country, the new policy will actually stigmatize African-American children—while validating habits of speech that bar them from the cultural mainstream and decent jobs.

The New York Times, Editorial

Many scholars contend that toleration represents a superior approach to diversity. Thus, whereas many scholars now call for a theory of assimilation, others now call for a theory of toleration. Opponents of assimilation fear that the melting pot is really a smelting pot. In a now famous essay, "Democracy versus the Melting Pot," Horace Kallen (1915) said that "What is inalienable in the life of mankind is its intrinsic positive quality—its psycho-physical inheritance. Men may change their clothes, their politics, their wives, their religions, their philosophies, to a greater or lesser extent; they cannot change their grandfathers. Jews or Poles or Anglo-Saxons, in order to cease being Jews or Poles or Anglo-Saxons, would have to cease to be" (p. 190). Kallen saw tolerance as vital to protecting such *real* differences as ethnicity. We have also seen that though Salins calls for a brand of assimilation that respects and relatively sustains cultural pluralism, his goal is to bring about a conversion to a certain religion. He wants homogeneity. He believes that conversion to a common religion is vital for unity and progress. In this way, the melting process seeks to curb the opportunity for new and possibly different ways of being.

Proponents of toleration stress metaphors that sustain differences. On the other hand, the common casting of assimilation and pluralism as either good or bad is believed to be an overly rigid dichotomy that unfairly exaggerates the differences between the different positions. Philip Gleason (1992), author of *Speaking of Diversity*, contends:

Both terms are figurative, rich and complex in implication; they can be interpreted in many different ways and can cover a wide range of social phenomena or policy options. In short, they are not mutually exclusive; rather they overlap and merge into each other. The reason they overlap is that each was intended by its originator to comprehend the full spectrum of tendencies in American society—the impulse to unity and the tendency toward multiplicity, the elements shared universally as well as the features that set people apart. The melting pot, to be sure, lays greater stress on *unum* than on *pluribus*, while pluralism reverses the emphasis; but both terms implicitly comprehend both ends of the polarity. (p. 42)

Those who favor *unum* stress assimilation and want a theory of assimilation, whereas those who favor *pluribus* stress toleration and want a theory of toleration. However, ambiguity about the virtues of toleration pervades the writings of its most vociferous proponents. This ambiguity is captured well in a recent book, *Is Multiculturalism Bad for Women*, edited by Joshua Cohen, Matthew Howard, and Martha Nussbaum (1999). Contributors respond to Susan Moller Okin's argument about a tension between feminism and multiculturalism. Okin argues that the protection of minority group rights often legitimizes practices—such as polygamy, arranged marriages of children, and clitoridectomy—that thwart the strivings of women. She believes that minority cultures that sanction such practices should be bound by the laws and values of liberalism that uphold gender equality.

Many of the contributors oppose Okin's position. Among other criticisms, she is accused of cultural chauvinism and gender colonialism. Bonnie Honig argues that liberalism undermines the collectivist spirit that is at the heart of feminism. She writes:

Liberalism's relentless individualism . . . feeds a privatizing, with-drawalist conception of citizenship that is at least tensely related to feminism's project of empowering women to act in concert to advance their own aims. If there is a question to be posed about whether feminism is well served by multiculturalism—and there surely is—there is just as surely a question to be posed about whether feminism is entirely well served by its association with liberalism. (p. 39)

Joseph Raz believes that Okin stereotypes minority cultures. Stereotyping obviously distorts any meaningful understanding of such cultures. It also masks, according to Faz, a deep hypocrisy: "We do not reject our culture when we find it replete with oppression and the violation of rights; we try to reform it. We should not assume the right to reject or condemn wholesale the cultures of groups within ours in similar cultures" (p. 97). Raz no doubt makes a valid point. Homi Bhabha also accuses Okin of distorting the complexity of non-Western peoples: "They are represented as having no local traditions of protest, no indigenous feminist movements, no sources of cultural and political contestation. . . . Her version of liberal feminism shares something of the patronizing and stereotyping attitudes of the patriarchal perspectives" (p. 82).

Bhikhu Parekh charges that Okin is working with an overly narrow definition of multiculturalism. Accommodation of minority cultures is merely a minor component of multiculturalism. According to Parekh:

> Pared down to its barest essentials and purged of the polemical exaggeration of its defenders and detractors, it represents the view that culture provides the necessary and inescapable context of human life, that all moral and political doctrines tend to reflect and universalize their cultural origins, that all cultures are partial and benefit from the insights of others, and that truly universal values can be arrived at only by means of an uncoerced and equal intercultural dialogue. (p. 74)

Parekh goes on to posit that "Multiculturalism deflates the absolutist pretensions of liberalism and requires it to acknowledge its contingent historical and cultural roots" (p. 74). However, although he criticizes Okin for uncritically accepting liberalism, he believes that multiculturalism ultimately expands liberalism and, in doing so, ends any tension between multiculturalism and feminism. He makes this point extremely well:

> We need instead a multicultural theory of liberalism that both cherishes and appreciates the limitations of the great liberal values, assigns them their proper but limited place in the moral world, and provides a framework of thought and action in which different cultures can cooperatively explore their differences and create a rich and lively community based on their respective insights. When allowed to flourish under the minimally necessary moral constraints, multiculturalism is likely to generate radically novel ways of conceptualizing and structuring intergender relations that cannot but deepen and broaden the hitherto somewhat parochial feminist sensibility. Far from being the enemy of women, it gives them the unique historical opportunity to pluralize and transform radically the universally hegemonic and boringly homogenous patriarchal culture that damages both women and men alike. (p. 75)

Other writings by prominent proponents of toleration reflect tensions about its virtues. Michael Walzer (1997), author of *On Toleration*, writes:

> I begin with the proposition that peaceful coexistence (of a certain sort: I am not writing here about the existence of masters and slaves) is

always a good thing. Not because people always in fact value it—they obviously don't. The sign of its goodness is that they are so strongly inclined to say that they value it: they can't justify themselves, to themselves or to one another, without endorsing the value of peaceful coexistence and of the life and liberty it serves. This is a fact about the moral world—at least in the limited sense that the burden of the argument falls on those who would reject these values. (p. 2)

Walzer believes that cultural associations and a narrow gap between rich and poor are necessary for the success of toleration. He admits that toleration is a tenuous notion that is dependent on stability. In other words, toleration is really an artifact of stability, which is to say that our foremost concern must be with forging and sustaining stability. Walzer gives us a secular understanding of diversity. He assumes that nothing is fundamentally existential or spiritual about diversity, or for that matter human beings. He also posits no theory of diversity. Accordingly, Walzer tells us nothing about how and why diversity is vital for both human and collective development. He sees diversity as something that must be managed, however tenuous the result will always be, through toleration.

No doubt the tenuous nature of toleration raises serious concerns. As Horton acknowledges, "What is clear though is that any liberal theory in which toleration has a central place must offer some account of why it is valuable. It is not an obvious or uncontroversial good." The enormous effort put forth—accepting differences that are believed to be morally abominable—to sustain what is after all a tenuous result eventually gives way. Stanley Fish (1997) observes:

[T]he trouble with stipulating tolerance as your first principle is that you cannot possibly be faithful to it because sooner or later the culture whose core values you are tolerating will reveal itself to be intolerant at the same core; that is, the distinctiveness that marks it as unique and self-defining will resist the appeal of moderation or incorporation into the larger whole. Confronted with a demand that it surrender its viewpoint or enlarge it to include the practices of its natural enemies—other religions, other races, other genders, other classes—a beleaguered culture will fight back with everything from discriminatory legislation to violence. (pp. 382-383)

History bears sufficient testimony to this point. Toleration is seen to demand too much of us and for no apparent benefit, and, as a result, when the opportunity appears, dominant groups seek to oppress minority groups. On the other hand, Walzer offers no objective framework that speaks to what differences should be tolerated. He is slippery on this point. He acknowledges that "To argue that different groups and/or individuals should be allowed to coexist in peace is not to argue that every actual or imaginable difference should be tolerated. . . . The toleration of problematic practices varies across the different regimes in a complex way, and the judgments we make of the variance are likely to be similarly complex" (p. 6). It is doubtful that many persons would call for the toleration of slavery and ethnic cleansing. These are easy examples, as Walzer must well know. What about, say, homosexuality, or even capitalism? Interestingly, although Walzer believes that stability through narrowing the gap between rich and poor is vital for toleration, even the most vociferous proponents of capitalism admit that capitalism is antithetical to this goal. It is actually responsible for exacerbating the gap that Walzer fears most. Consequently, why should capitalism be tolerated?

The fact of the matter is that toleration is without any theoretical or moral ground. What Walzer passes off as a moral proposition is nothing of the sort. His own admission that toleration will always be a tenuous framework reveals that no relation is assumed between toleration and human or collective development. Walzer makes no pretension about toleration being something that is related to our moral development or something even existential and spiritual in origin.

Other prominent scholarly treatments of toleration also make no such pretension. In an essay titled "The Difficulty of Tolerance", T. M. Scanlon (1996) writes, "Tolerance involves a more attractive and appealing relation between opposing groups. Any society, no matter how homogenous, will include people who disagree about how to live and about what they want their society to be like. . . . Given that there must be disagreement, and that those who disagree must live together, is it not better, if possible, to have these disagreements contained within a framework of mutual respect?" (p. 230). Moreover, Nick Fotion and Gerard Elfstrom (1992), authors of *Toleration*, admit that "It [toleration] is not a morally pivotal concept in the sense that no moral principle is generated and no moral system created simply by understanding it. Instead, engaging in normative ethics on any level . . . requires appeal to moral principles that apparently have little or nothing directly to do with toleration" (p. 151).

The fact that proponents of toleration admit that nothing is fundamentally moral about toleration raises a moral paradox. On one hand, toleration demands that what is being asked to be tolerated must at least be tolerable, which means that our capacity for toleration must be enlarged to become tolerant so as to cover everything that is potentially tolerable. Thus, to become tolerant, and presumably less bigoted, narrow-minded persons must become less judgmental and biased, which is to say, they must relax their convictions to their own morals, beliefs, and truths. However, doing so undermines differences, for our morals, beliefs, and truths are diluted without any deep conviction. What then becomes the virtues of such morals, truths, and beliefs to begin with? Yet, on the other hand, toleration demands the highest levels of toleration—a superseding belief that toleration is decent, good, and moral.

Toleration encourages moral relativism—all is good except that which is abominable. We gain nothing—besides survival, which apparently Walzer sees as a victory—from tolerating differences that are believed to be wrong. Walzer struggles to tell us why doing so is morally good. He seems to know that such an argument lacks theoretical ground. Integral to the psychology of being dominant is the belief that you will always be strong and the Other forever weak. It is this kind of ego that most often perverts human decency. So why toleration?

Ryzard Legutko (1994) is convinced that the concept is theoretically vacuous. He calls for the end of toleration. Legutko believes that strong cultural attachments block rootlessness, instability, and identity crises, all which he believes are the root causes of tribalism. He writes, "There is certainly some correlation between self-confidence, deriving from an awareness of the opportunity to rely on norms believed to be stable and valid, and civility, with which one may approach other points of view. . . . For this reason, well-integrated communities, just as well-integrated individuals, are better partners of coexistence than those whose sense of integration has been weakened" (p. 622). On the other hand, the cultural attachment that Legutko celebrates—the translation of which is deification—is what makes for tribalism by suppressing the natural evolution of differences and, by that, the suppression of conflict. Without either diversity or conflict, systems atrophy.

Robert Weissberg (1998), author of *Political Tolerance*, wants to rescue toleration from multiculturalism radicals and bad theory. Though a proponent of toleration, Weissberg actually wants less of it. He argues that calls for unrestricted toleration is based on faulty premises, foremost of which is that unlimited toleration is politically and morally virtuous, and that our society has a low threshold for diversity. Weissberg contends that toleration must be grounded in a fixed set of guiding principles that simply forbids certain practices that threaten the common good. He writes: "The forceful repression of political ideas and groups, even if not an immediate physical threat or a clear violation of criminal law, can be reasonably defended, even in a democracy. . . . We are not talking of mere rebuke or condemnation, we are vindicating state *coercion*" (p. 77). Yet, "There is no neat formula, nor can one be furnished. Searching for an effortless, logical, abstract way to establish the point at which a democratic group crosses the line and transforms itself into a subversive conspiracy is foolhardy" (p. 108).

Weissberg contends that his guiding principles offer no guarantees of full communal legitimacy for homosexuals. He believes that society possesses the obligation to govern public morality and decorum. He prescribes that the majority of the citizens determine what is public morality and decorum. Weissberg contends that what makes full communal legitimacy for homosexuals tenuous is that the majority simply rejects it. Apparently, homosexuals should be happy that the majority accepts discreet homosexual behavior. After all, "Being gay could be viewed as no different from indulging in a risky weakness, a predilection akin to alcoholism and drug addiction. Forced therapy to cure those apprehended for succumbing to the temptation of risky homosexual eroticism is conceivable, just as drug addicts caught in criminal acts are occasionally forced into therapy" (p. 174). In sum, might is everything. Weissberg has apparently forgotten that this political formulation has long legitimized the most virulent forms of racism and sexism. It is also the framework that made for the Holocaust.

The premise of unrestricted toleration is also unfair. Weissberg never accounts for the origins of this premise. He conflates being highly tolerant with being unrestrictedly tolerant, which is nothing but theoretical mischief. He uses unrestricted toleration as a red herring: No proponent of multiculturalism wants unrestricted toleration. Even the usual targets of most opponents of multiculturalism want to end certain cultural and political practices. It is the arbitrary desire to end certain practices but yet sustain others—as already been discussed—that bedevils the politics of Fish and company. The point has long been made that Fish and company have no moral or theoretical ground to make any meaningful distinction; thus the criticism is hypocrisy. Weissberg is now trying to say that Fish and company have committed heresy rather than hypocrisy. But hypocrisy trumps heresy. Further, system theory, again, posits that systems need both diversity and homogeneity to affirm life. All systems seek to attain a union of both. Systems disallow unrestricted toleration.

Setting up unrestricted toleration as a red herring allows Weissberg to play directly to our deep fear and suspicion of our humanity. Whereas the notion of highly tolerant connotes reason and restraint, that of unrestricted tolerance connotes promiscuity and chaos. His contention that a certain amount of repression is vital for the making of the good society rests squarely on this sentiment. He knows how much our relation to each other is shaped by this fear. Weissberg is spared having to account for the validity of the bedrock assumption that undergirds his argument. The result, however, besides bad theory, is bad politics. In reinforcing our deep distrust and suspicion of our humanity, Weissberg further legitimizes the status quo. Then again, according to his postscript, this was always his ambition. Interestingly, the postscript also posits that the howls of derision against the Oakland resolution is a good sign of the growing frustration with blanket tolerance.

The reality is that toleration—as with assimilation—is also born of our distrust and suspicion of our humanity. It, too, is born of fear. It is for this reason that Walzer sees survival as a compelling enough reason for toleration. We supposedly need to understand that without toleration the strong will destroy the weak. Everything about our being is reduced to surviving, and morality is anything that promotes functional relations between different peoples. The matter is purely utilitarian. What also makes toleration attractive is the belief that the world is without any universal moral calculus. It is our responsibility to find our own moral codes. Toleration also reflects a fear that moral codes will descend from on high and coercively obliterate the diversity of all peoples. Yet what makes toleration most pernicious is the excusing of dysfunctional behavior, specifically behaviors that engender and sustain the status quo. Under the guise of respect for cultural differences, human beings, through toleration, can avoid engaging the world dialogically, thereby sustaining the status quo. The result is that of a few blocking the many from creating new and different ways of being. Toleration spares us from dealing with the fear that is naturally bound up with the ambiguity of the world. It undercuts the catalyst—that is, ambiguity—vital for new ways of being and experiencing the world. In this way, toleration makes for oppression by thwarting moral development, which is entwined with the forging of deep and meaningful human relations. In short, toleration blocks scrutiny of domination. As Dwight Boyd (1996) points out: "Thus, claiming that one will/should tolerate some view *appears* to be aimed at some kind of equality, when in fact it assumes and maintains a position of relative power from which it can be done. . . . When tolerance is the only moral coin in the context of diversity, the norm of the dominant view wins by default" (p. 623). By blocking scrutiny of domination, toleration undercuts diversity.

Toleration is neither dialogical nor transformational. It is without existential and spiritual origins. The promotion of toleration reinforces the hegemony of the secular. Toleration legitimizes our distrust and suspicion of our humanity. It legitimizes human relations woven with fear, distrust, and suspicion. Toleration is about devising schemes to deal with and accept our fear, distrust, and suspicion of the other. It undercuts the possibility of new ways of being. In being nondialogical and nontransformational, toleration blocks scrutiny of the worldview that sustains the status quo. Finally, toleration promotes closed systems. Such systems seek no engagement with other systems. We find an aversion to growth and transformation. The point is that an objective moral and theoretical calculus—with existential and spiritual and moral

underpinnings—exists in the form of system theory that rejects toleration as a theoretically valid way of dealing with diversity. No theoretical
ground exists to fear diversity. But the diversity that is vital for growth
and development is by no means arbitrary. Discursive and nondiscursive practices that thwart our existential and spiritual strivings are dysfunctional. The goal is to seek the end of dysfunctional practices and
beliefs noncoercively. Other means engender aggression and other dysfunctional outcomes that block the possibility of transformation. Only
dialogical action is moral.

SUMMARY AND CONCLUSION

The negotiation of differences continues to bedevil organizational
life. Diversity is commonly referred to as a double-edged sword.
On the one hand, research consistently correlates diversity with
creativity and superior decision making (e.g., Watson, Kumar, &
Michaelson, 1993). However, on the other hand, diversity is associated
with higher turnover rates, less job satisfaction levels, higher levels of
deviancy, higher levels of absenteeism, and less-integrated collectives
(e.g., Wagner, Pfeffer, & O'Reilly, 1984). In a recent comprehensive
review of the organizational diversity literature, Milliken and Martins
(1996) posit:

> One of the most striking and most important findings of research on
> diversity is that groups that are diverse have lower levels of member
> satisfaction and higher rates of turnover than more homogenous
> groups. This is true across a wide range of types of diversity, includ-
> ing age, gender, racial/ethnic background, and tenure. Similarly, peo-
> ple who are different from others in their groups tend to be less satis-
> fied, and individuals who are unlike their supervisors on these char-
> acteristics tend to receive lower performance evaluations. The consis-
> tency of these findings suggests the presence of a systematic problem,
> namely that groups and organizations will act systematically to drive
> out individuals who are different from the majority. (p. 420)

Buzzanell (1994, 1995, 1999), Allen (1995, 1996, 1998), Collins
(1991), Orbe (1998), Allen, Orbe, and Refugia (1999), and other scholars
give us compelling testimony and insight about the experiences of
women and minority persons that explain this antipathy to differences.
Milliken and Martins (1996), however, speculate about whether organizations can afford the trade-off between the benefits and costs of diversity: "If so, are there ways in which organizations can perform a balancing

act between the costs and benefits of diversity? On the other hand, is it possible for organizations to get the best of both worlds by minimizing the affective costs and maximizing the cognitive and symbolic benefits of diversity?" (p. 421). These are the questions that organizational scholars are increasingly asking as diversity programs seem to have no significant effect on organizational practices (Ableson, 1999). The matter is compounded by the fact that organizations are being forced to deal with increasing levels of differences, through emerging world markets, labor resources, and technology.

The problem is that organizational scholars are working with assumptions that make for a narrow understanding of diversity. As discussed throughout this book, diversity is supposedly about *differences*, such as race, ethnicity, gender, and so forth. Organizations are assuming that the addition of differences brings about diversity. This narrow view of diversity favors organizational interests by blocking scrutiny of organizational practices, such as hierarchy, that block diversity. But this narrow understanding has been accepted uncritically by organizational scholars from popular discourses about diversity found in the wider cultural and social environment. Also accepted uncritically are the popular theoretical schemes to deal with diversity and differences. Consequently, the organizational literature reflects the confusion, conflict, hostility, and misunderstanding found in popular discourses about diversity.

Organizational scholars are no doubt committed to tapping the virtues of diversity; the benefits are simply too compelling to surrender. It is also understood that organizations have at least to deal productively with a world that is increasingly heterogenous. In short, organizations look at diversity in terms of practicality. Yet diversity seems to be resisting practical solutions. Organizational scholars have yet to find a practical solution that maximizes benefits and minimizes costs. Consequently, most organizations face a bind, on the one hand confronting a world that is increasingly heterogenous and different, on the other, unwilling to end practices and structures that thwart diversity.

To look at diversity as an artifact of union moves diversity from the realm of practicality to one of morality. Diversity transcends concerns of benefits and costs. It no longer becomes a matter of whether organizations can afford the trade-off between the benefits and the costs of diversity, can find practical solutions, or can maximize benefits and minimize costs. Union deepens our understanding of diversity. To look at diversity as an artifact of union entwines diversity with organizing and being; diversity is thereby politicized. It is about ending domination and subordination. Diversity evolves with the end of hierarchy. It is about affirming the potentiality of life. It demands a risking of life, a commitment to transforming our consciousness of the world. Diversity as union also undermines the status quo. The end of hierarchy represents a redistribution of resources and power. Diversity as union locates diversity within the consciousness of the world. This is how union morally problematizes diversity: It is through diversity that life is affirmed and human beings help with the completion of the world. Diversity is a gift that human beings give to the world.

We could have used the Oakland situation to foster a unity based on diversity, equality, and compassion. We missed this opportunity. Instead, what was taught—actually reinforced—to our children is that coercion and aggression are the best means to deal with differences. Our children learned nothing about empathy and compassion. We reinforced the belief that human beings are amoral, aexistential, and aspiritual beings who are devoid of any striving to develop deep and meaningful human relations. A consciousness was reinforced. In the end, no amount of diversity will be responsible for disunity and civil disharmony. What will be responsible is a consciousness that engenders fear, distrust, competition, and maintains a deep suspicion of our humanity. Unless a new consciousness emerges, neither assimilation nor toleration can redeem us.

We now turn our attention to how the notion of human beings as existential and spiritual beings expand our understanding of culture. Indeed, no discussion of diversity is complete without a discussion of culture—a phenomenon that continues to bedevil discourses about diversity in the United States. The popular view is that diversity is about the negotiation of different cultures. All sides of the theoretical and political spectrum treat culture as a constant: We hear about black culture, white culture, gay culture, and so forth. Scholars spend enormous resources studying the features of different cultures and how they are different. The findings are always interesting and fascinating. This work has no doubt brought us to the realization that cultures do have real differences and that such differences should be respected, even celebrated. Traditional proponents of diversity focus on sustaining and protecting our different cultures in the belief that the obliteration of different cultures dehumanizes us. Consequently, the primary obligation of a civilized society is to protect the cultures of other peoples.

We have also seen that traditional opponents of diversity look at the matter differently. It is assumed that cultural pluralism threatens the stability of U.S. society. Such a position assumes that peoples of different cultures will resist assimilation and this will ultimately make for deadly conflict when such peoples are forced to deal with each other. Differences are seen as the root of tribal conflict. Consequently, opponents contend that the continued prosperity of U.S. society depends on assimilation rather than toleration, and on a curbing of peoples from different cultures, particularly those which many commentators have no qualms referring to as *inferior*. It is also believed that inferior cultures will eventually infect U.S. culture, which is assumed to be the only culture capable of affording any meaningful kind of cultural pluralism. We have already seen that many opponents of diversity claim that multiculturalism is uniquely a phenomenon of Western civilization.

I wish to get beyond the notion of culture as a constant. This popular view of culture assumes that cultures bound us. Both proponents and opponents of multiculturalism use this dominant understanding of culture to sustain a politics and ethics of separation. When the focus is on differences, the status quo ultimately wins. Both sides admit that any negotiation of cultural differences is perilous. Even the most vociferous proponents of toleration do not sanction cultures that practice slavery, discrimination, and so forth. On the other hand, proponents of assimilation admit that assimilation emasculates differences. The end result of both positions is always a solution that lacks harmony, reinforcing the view that the unity/diversity problem is unsolvable. This view reinforces the belief that human beings are aexistential and aspiritual and amoral beings and that no potential harmony exists between us and the world. In my view, this belief further legitimizes the secular hegemony. I focus on the enabling rather than bounding nature of cultures.

I view culture as an artifact of our existential and spiritual strivings. It is an artifact of questing for meaning. In locating the origin of culture in our existential and spiritual striving for meaning creation, I also aim to push forward the potential of communication theory to make significant contributions to our understanding of culture. I contend that cultures possesses an existential and spiritual potentiality that recursively expands our understanding of the world and each other. I focus on the universals that undergird all cultures. Such universals are equally as fascinating as our differences, meaning that a focus on universals by no means comes at the cost of downplaying differences. In fact, attention to such universals expands our understanding of the origins of differences. I aim to show how a view of culture as existential and spiritual makes for a politics and ethics of union. We will find that regardless of our cultural differences, all cultures are subject to the parameters of the world, or of the ethics that are entwined with life and transcend our politics. This ethics commits all cultures to a universal set of practices, and through such a commitment the possibility exists of union through cultural diversity. Cultures unwilling to maintain harmony with the ethics of this world are doomed.

5

On Ways
of Being

[Young people] use it [Ebonics] with great vibrancy. It is the language of freedom. It is the language of joy.
 Richard Wright, Sociolinguist, Howard University

It [Ebonics] would dumb down their abilities. It would make them the laughingstock among Americans and the linguistic pariahs on the English-speaking world stage; and it would isolate them from others far more perversely than the worst Southern sheriff or most ardent white racist ever could.
 Georgine Anne Geyer, *Chicago Tribune*

This [Ebonics] will not help the students become doctors or lawyers or help them get into the University of California. . . . This will do a disservice to the students.
 Delaine Eastin, Superintendent of Public Education, California

It is a racist affront against people who have struggled for decades to be a part of the American fiber.
 Steven Gooden, Honorary Youth Chairperson, Republican National Convention, San Diego

Popular definitions of culture posit no existential and spiritual assumptions about the origins of culture. We study culture as a phenomenon of transmission and representation. The following definitions show this plainly:

> Culture is created through communication. Culture is the set of stable consensual frames in a social system. . . . Culture is the active, interpretive process by which individuals create frames for meaningful relationships. Culture is created in the course of communication between the co-participants: meaning in a culture is just the extent to which communicating communities co-regulate stable themes of information. (Fogel, 1993)

> Culture consists of the abstract values, beliefs, and perceptions that lie behind people's behavior. . . . They are shared by members of a society, and when acted on, produce behavior considered to be acceptable within that society. (Haviland, 1993)

> Culture is . . . a pattern of basic assumptions—invented, discovered, or developed by a given group as it learns to cope with its problems of external adaption and internal integration—that has worked well enough to be considered valid and, therefore, to be taught to new members as the correct way to perceive, think, and feel in relation to those problems. (Schein, 1985)

No doubt culture is about ways of being. It reflects our habits of being, our values, beliefs, and so forth. But why culture? Popular understandings of culture view human beings as purely secular beings with no spiritual relation to the world and each other. Accordingly, though most definitions of culture give us rich and compelling descriptions of human activity and collective behavior, nothing existential or spiritual is assumed about the origins and purposes of culture.

The secular thrust that characterizes popular understandings of culture can arguably be traced to the early scholars who formalized the modern study of culture. It was assumed that our humanity was purely the sum of our discursive and material practices. The object of study was understanding how such practices fashion and constrain our humanity. As Brenda Dervin (1991) explains: "Borrowing from anthropology, we [communication scholars] have conceptualized culture primarily as a static structure embodying rules, norms, positions, rituals, and so on. The culture-structure is seen as exerting a transmission-like force on the individuals within it. Our understanding of cultures focuses on differences in these structures, which results have shown are at best modest and at worst highly changeable" (p. 64). Our humanity was seen as a kind of cultural molding block, devoid of any agency or existential and spiritual strivings. According to Fromm (1973), "The study of primitive peoples has discovered such a variety of customs, values, feelings, and thoughts that many anthropologists arrived at the concept that man is born as a blank sheet of paper on which each culture writes its text" (p. 247). What emerged from this orientation is a preoccupation with the discursive and material practices that supposedly fashion our being. The human dimension was downplayed; instead, the focus was on structures and institutions and traditions.

A secular orientation still frames much of our understanding of culture. It is assumed that nothing exists beyond the discursive and material realm. We are told—as already been extensively discussed—that no objective comparison of cultures is possible. Cultures supposedly limit our being. We are framed within cultures. We find a fascination with *differences*. Supposedly, this is a world without universals. It is assumed that human beings have no common humanity. Nothing supposedly binds us to each other. Supposedly, no objective moral ground *really* exists to treat human beings of different cultures humanely and decently. In this way, our dominant secular understanding of culture constrains moral action and undermines prudential conduct (Cherwitz & Hikins, 1990). It engenders cultural enclaves and also fosters the reifying and deifying of cultures by focusing exclusively on our cultural differences. The result is a secular understanding of culture that affords no calculus to ground an ethics and politics that moves beyond differences. Consequently, any ethics and politics that aim to move beyond the status quo must look beyond the cultural to the universal.

Universal Grammar is a universal; our proclivity for union is a universal; our proclivity for transparency is also a universal. Universals reflect our existential and spiritual strivings as well as our ability to transcend our many differences. Universals also expand our understanding of differences by drawing our attention to the reality that this is a world of differences. In what follows I discuss our *striving to transcend the present* and our capacity and *proclivity for meaning creation* as universals. Together, both expand our understanding of differences and diversity.

OUR SPIRITUAL QUEST

The Ebonics controversy is, finally and most importantly, a fight not only apparently about language, but in fact really about language—that is, language as an instrument of influence and social control. . . . I think this will turn out to be the major political issue of the pre-millennium: the determination of who controls language, makes meaning, makes the words that can be used for public discourse, establishes the modality of that public discourse, and determines as a result who and what can and should be listened to and taken seriously. Language may be no more that exhalations of air, but whoever control language has political control—power.

Robin Lakoff, Professor of Linguistics, University of California, Berkeley

Cultures do fashion our understanding of the world. However, on the other hand, history evidences progress. We do transform and abolish cultures. We are *culturing* beings. History compellingly show us continuously transcending the present, creating and reinventing cultures, structures, and institutions. We are constantly pushing against the status quo. We seem bent on ending the forces and structures that thwart evolution and transformation. Robert Torrance (1994), author of *The Spiritual Quest*, compellingly theorizes that human beings possess a spiritual quest that represents a striving to transcend our present historical and material location. He describes this as "the process through which our evolving humanity, resolutely transgressing the continual impasse of the given, steps repeatedly forth in quest of the transformative and always future unknown" (p. 294). It also represents a "strenuous search for an objective knowledge—knowledge of a reality beyond yet inseparable from the perceiving self—that enlarges both the individual seeker and those with whom she shares the results of her exploration" (p. 284). Torrance looks at our spiritual quest as the striving that propels evolution and transformation. It represents the forces that push against the obstacles that hinder life. "In either case, every hindrance is potentially a point of departure, every aporia an opportunity to renew the quest for an object that cannot be known . . . even when found, since it is continually being transformed, and only thus can satisfy the human need for a transcendence that has no terminus this side of death" (p. 293).

Communication is an artifact of our spiritual quest. According to Torrance (1994), "Communication, like life . . . consciousness, and the spiritual quest that strives to transcend their given limits, is thus a self-transformative process that progresses, by unpredictable actualizations of multiple possibilities, through liminal indeterminacy toward an evolving goal" (p. 271). This spiritual quest reveals that human beings are by no means passive to the world. It undermines the claim that our humanity is purely a discursive creation. It reveals a natural aspiration to transcend the present, a proclivity to grow and develop. Our spiritual questing affirms transformation and evolution as the order of the world. In this way, this spiritual quest provides a compelling explanation of the transformation that all cultures undergo. It makes active our understanding of culture and history. This spiritual quest also foregrounds the human element. It shows human beings—within a spiritual context—acting and shaping the world. Most of all, this spiritual quest reaffirms the notion that this is a moral world and stresses the potentiality of human beings for morality. It points to a common morality that resides within *all* human beings.

OUR MEANING QUEST

> While using Ebonics may seem well-meaning, it is not well-serving. The whole concept is even worse now because children must be trained to survive and compete in a global environment that requires them to expand their communication skills at a minimum.
> Adrienne Washington, Columnist, *The Washington Times*

It is generally agreed that our cultures reflect our beliefs, values, assumptions, truths, and so forth. Cultures reflect ways of being, our different ways of looking and experiencing the world. But what does the nature of beliefs, hopes, assumptions, and values tell us about being human? Why do all human beings—regardless of race, ethnicity, gender, and so forth—have (though different) beliefs, values, truths, assumptions, and so forth? What explains this commonality and universality? The reason is that such notions are mechanisms that allow for meaning creation and mutual understanding. The fact that all human beings have a common set of mechanisms to aid meaning creation affirms our proclivity and capacity for meaning creation as a universal. Our meaning creation mechanisms are only descriptively different. We are bound by a common set of mechanisms.

Yet, popular understandings of culture focus exclusively on our different discursive and material practices. We are fixated on our cultural differences. We focus disproportionately on the occasions of cultural conflict rather than cultural harmony. We have convinced ourselves that our differences damn us to conflict and disharmony with peoples of different cultures. It is popularly assumed that these cultural differences hinder deep and meaningful relations between peoples of different cultures. Accordingly, traditional opponents of multiculturalism contend that the focus must be on preserving the stability and integrity of our own traditions, institutions, and cultures.

It is human to want the low ambiguity that our cultures afford us through a common set of beliefs, values, and so forth. The anxiety that ambiguity produces leads to a natural aversion to peoples and cultures that threaten our homogeneity and stability with different beliefs, values, and so on. We fear the ambiguity (read chaos and disunity) that such peoples elicit in us. We come to prefer equilibrium rather than disequilibrium, homogeneity rather than diversity, order rather than chaos, continuity rather than discontinuity. To this end, many cultures eventually develop beliefs, hopes, fears, and values that seek to limit ambiguity and disequilibrium. Rigid and complex structures appear to block all ambiguity and disequilibrium. *Institutional man* appears. We begin to hear ominous warnings about the clash of civilizations—as in the case of Samuel Huntington—and the urgent need to vigorously defend our institutions and traditions. We also begin to deify our traditions and institutions—fearing that the end of both threatens chaos and disunity. We find an ethics and politics of separation rather than union.

Universals make for a different ethics and politics. Entwined with our need to bring meaning to bear on the world is a natural aversion to the world's ambiguity. On the other hand, seeking to end all ambiguity only fosters dysfunctionality, insofar as ambiguity catalyzes meaning creation and allows us to look at the world anew. In this way, all cultures need ambiguity, which is to say that all cultures need disequilibrium and disunity. All cultures have to allow for continuity and discontinuity, evolution and transformation, order and chaos. The end of ambiguity is death. Universals undercut any moral argument that legitimizes the end of diversity and disequilibrium. In this way, universals give us moral ground by drawing our attention to a world that is moral.

Universals also supply us with a calculus to distinguish between ethical and unethical communication. Ethical communication allows for evolution and transformation (Thayer, 1973). It allows for the open expression of conflict and disequilibrium. It focuses on creating a context that allows for both the evolution and devolution of meanings. Ethical communication is characterized by high levels of affirmation. It is dialogical. Dialogical communication assumes that our becoming is entwined with that of the world. Anything that adversely affects our becoming also adversely affects the becoming of the world. As Martin Buber (1994) explains:

> That peoples can no longer carry on authentic dialogue with one another is not only the most acute symptom of the pathology of our time, it is also that which most urgently makes a demand on us. I believe, despite all, that the peoples in this hour can enter into dialogue, into a genuine dialogue with one another. In a genuine dialogue each of the partners, even when he stands in opposition to the other, heeds, affirms, and confirms his opponent as an existing other. Only so can conflict certainly not be eliminated from the world, but be humanly arbitrated and led towards its overcoming. (p. 311)

Dialogical communication reflects a deep sensitivity to human fragility. It aims to affirm and renew life. Conversely, the effects of unethical communication are real and debilitating. In blocking the evolution of empathy, compassion, trust, and so forth, unethical communication blocks our becoming fully human and our ability to develop deep and meaningful human relations. The effects of conflict suppression are real and perilous. In thwarting diversity, conflict suppression undercuts the formation of deep and meaningful relations. The point is that universals accent a consciousness that embraces ambiguity and disequilibrium as vital to life. Universals also reveal that, regardless of our best efforts, the consciousness of this world rejects the preservation of cultures and civilizations. It is an exercise that is doomed to futility.

LANGUAGE AND COMMUNICATION

There's nothing worse a school board could do to ruin a child's self-esteem than to create a special language for blacks. It's degrading. It reinforces negative stereotypes.
    S. Carter, Student, University of Texas

Ebonics was not created by black culture. It was created by a deteriorating school system that was ill-equipped or failed to teach the proper use and mastery of the English language.
    Kirk McDaniel, *Black Enterprise*

I consider this institutionalized dysfunction. . . . Our aspiration has to be excellence in English. I would not vote to expose our children under the guise that you are imparting something of value. I do not go along. . . . I understand and applaud cultural and linguistic diversity, but I reject all arguments that carry political correctness to the extreme of promoting anything other than English as our official language. . . . The only place for Ebonics is in the streets. We don't need it in the classroom; we need to rescue kids from Ebonics.
    Eldridge Cleaver, Founding Member and Minister of
    Information, Black Panther Party

Believing that culture fashions our humanity—the way that popular definitions of culture suggest—assumes that language shapes our thoughts. In scholarly terms, this is the famous Sapir-Whorf hypothesis. One effect of this hypothesis is an emphasis on expunging language of racist and sexist words and phrases. Many legal scholars even call for the criminilization of certain kinds of speech. Interestingly, both opponents and proponents of cultural diversity support this hypothesis. For example, Schmidt (1997) contends that "this theory sheds some light on why the world's greatest documents of human freedom and liberty were first enshrined in the English language. . . . It is all but impossible to have freedom of discussion, political compromise, or dissent when a country's language is devoid of such concepts" (p. 124). Yet, the reality is that the Sapir-Whorf hypothesis masks our capacity and striving to bring meaning to bear on the world. It nouns rather than verbs our understanding of communication. We are cast as receptacles rather than actors.

The Sapir-Whorf hypothesis also masks our proclivity and capacity for communication by reducing thoughts and emotions to language and our cognitive schemes to mere receptacles of language. In *The Language Instinct*, Steven Pinker (1994) writes the following about the Sapir-Whorf hypothesis:

> The idea that thought is the same thing as language is an example of what can be called a conventional absurdity: a statement that goes against all common sense but that everyone believes because they dimly recall having heard it somewhere and because it is so pregnant with meaning. . . . Sometimes it is not easy to find any words that properly convey a thought. When we hear or read, we usually remember the gist, not the exact words, so there has to be such a thing as a gist that is not the same as a bunch of words. And if thoughts depended on words, how could a new word ever be coined? How could a child learn a word to begin with? How could translation from one language to another be possible? (pp. 57-58)

The Sapir-Whorf hypothesis clashes with the reality that human beings are constantly creating and reinventing communication. New meanings reflect new ways of experiencing the world. In turn, new experiences make for new meanings of the world and each other. New meanings are born out of our engagement with the ambiguity that pervades the world. The Sapir-Whorf hypothesis assumes that our experiences are set, our meanings are set. It assumes that meanings are transmitted rather than negotiated, that experiences are shared rather than recreated. Our reality rejects the stability that the Sapir-Whorf hypothesis assumes. Our experiences of the world can never be confined to a fixed set of meanings, codes, and symbols. Communication occurs within gaps and spaces. It is within the dialectical play between chaos and order, stability and displacement, volition and structures, and so on, that meaning is created and negotiated. Communication is linear and nonlinear, negotiational and transactional. No meaning is ever devoid of ambiguity. Consequently, what requires changing is our relation to the world and each other rather than criminalizing words and symbols. To end racism and sexism ultimately requires changing our relation to the world and each other rather than merely ending certain words. It is after all only human beings and relationships that matter.

Pinker believes that a universal set of cognitive schemes governs our thoughts, similar to how a Universal Grammar governs languages. He believes that those cognitive schemes are beyond language. Pinker posits a hypothesis about a language of thought that is universal and a priori to language. He refers to this universal language of thought as *mentalese*. Pinker (1994) explains:

> People do not think in English or Chinese or Apache; they think in a language of thought. This language of thought probably looks a bit like all these languages; presumably it has symbols for concepts, and arrangement of symbols that correspond to who did what to whom. . . . But compared with any given language, mentalese must be richer in some ways and simpler in others. . . . On the other hand, mentalese must be simpler than spoken languages; conversation-specific words and constructions (like a and the) are absent, and information about pronouncing words, or even ordering them, is unnecessary. . . . But to get these languages of thought to subserve reasoning properly, they would have to look much more like each other than either one does to its spoken counterpart, and it is likely that they are the same: a universal mentalese. (pp. 81-82)

This notion of human beings having a universal language of thought is compelling. It shows cultures being organically constrained by nature—universally. It seems to further support the view that human beings do possess existential and spiritual attributes that transcend cultures. But Pinker looks at the matter differently. He discusses neither worldviews nor meaning. He also never acknowledges our distinct proclivity and capacity to bring meaning to bear on the world. He believes that language is purely an artifact of natural selection forces. In this way, both Pinker and proponents of the Sapir-Whorf hypothesis neglect both our distinct capacity and striving to bring meaning to bear on the world and how meaning creation recursively fashions our humanity. Consequently, neither Pinker nor proponents of the Sapir-Whorf hypothesis tells us anything substantive about the relation between communication, culture, and being.

The notions of a universal language of thought and that of Universal Grammar both bound our ways of being. But this bounding is of an enabling kind: It is this bounding that enables an unfolding of endless articulations of being. It is our proclivity for meaning, however, that makes for different worldviews and cultures. Communication makes creation the order of the world and it is our relation to the world that sets our relation to our languages rather than our languages that set our relation to the world. Communication precedes and exceeds language. Pinker conflates language with communication. We have already seen that this is a mistake that many theorists commonly make. Pinker (1994) writes:

> Thinking of language as an instinct inverts the popular wisdom, especially as it has been passed down in the canon of the humanities and social sciences. Language is no more a cultural invention than is upright posture. It is not a manifestation of a general capacity to use symbols. . . . Though language is a magnificent ability unique to Homo sapiens among living species, it does not call for sequestering the study of humans from the domain of biology, for a magnificent ability unique to a particular living species is far from unique in the animal kingdom. . . . In nature's talent show we are simply a species of primate with our own act, a knack for communicating information about who did what to whom by modulating the sounds we make when we exhale. (pp. 18-19)

Pinker assumes that communication is informational. In actuality, however, communication is relational and ontological. It represents the creation and negotiation of meaning between dyads and or collectives. According to Stanley Deetz (1995):

> Communication . . . refers to the social processes by which meanings, identities, psychological states, social structures, and the various means of the contact of the organization with the environment are both produced, reproduced, or changed. In both its constitutive and reproductive modes, communication processes are central to how perceptions, meanings, routines are held in common. (p. 90)

The creation and negotiation of meaning is by no means dependent on codes. This is what makes communication a uniquely human phenomenon. Communication as both an existential and spiritual phenomenon reflects our distinct capacity to bring meaning to bear on the world. Communication is the constitutive element of being human. It chisels and sculpts our humanity. It is through communication that human beings are humanized, which is to say that a sacred relation exists between being human, communication, and culture. Meanings belong both to human beings and the perspectives that our cultures allow, which means that all meanings have objective and subjective origins. According to Richard Cherwitz and Thomas Darwin (1995), the "tendency to approach meaning as a function of either objects or language use . . . leads to an inability to account for the simultaneous capacity of language to be constrained by and shape objects" (p. 17). Cherwitz and Darwin correctly contend that meaning is fundamentally relational:

> The relational constituent of context . . . underscores the importance of *connotative parameters* to meaning. To be sure, awareness of one's perspective—i.e., one's culture, ideology or other vantage point—is necessary to the discernment of meaning. What we typically call mythic, ideological and cultural meanings, for instance, entail comprehension of more than just the denotative factors defining a given language; these meanings also are a function of contextual variables—variables that *perspectively* situate and locate communicators in time and space, influencing their comprehension of bodies in the world and the subsequent use of language. It must be emphasized that, while these unique perspectives account for different meanings . . . and subsequent disagreements among people, the *contexts* framing these perspectives are objectively instantiated. (p. 22, italics in original)

The objective/subjective nature of meaning demonstrates the virtues of our existential and spiritual strivings to transcend the present and for meaning creation. It is herein that the potentiality of cultures to foster diversity resides. We can probably best explain this by using an analogy of six persons looking at a building from various points. For discussion purposes, let us pretend that each point represents a different culture and thus possibly a different way of being.

The person who is looking at the building from a blimp in the sky no doubt has a different perspective from that of the person who is on the inside. In turn, this person on the inside has a different perspective of the building from that of any of the persons standing on each of the four sides. The building is no doubt real. It is objective. But our various positions delimit our perspectives and fashion our understanding of the building. Meaning is always relational. As Cherwitz and Darwin (1995) explain, "To suggest that meaning is based on the capacity of one body to mirror another . . . assumes that the bodies are unrelated and are categorically distinct. . . . Every particular in the world exhibits curious characteristics that emerge as a function of the relations in which the particular stands to other members of its context. . . . Uniqueness and dissimilarity are a function of differences—differences that exist because of the particular relationships obtaining within, between, and among bodies" (pp. 20-21). I am, on the other hand, by no means suggesting that all positions give equal understandings of the building. In fact, Phillips (1997) puts the matter nicely:

> None of us sprang up overnight . . . and all of us are simultaneously empowered and constrained by the cultural assumptions through which we have come to view the world. Knowing this—and knowing at the same time that there are many cultures—we cannot but see ourselves as partial, with our most certain convictions always open to subsequent revision. The equal respect we owe to people from other cultures is best expressed in assuming that they were similarly formed; that all of us have learned particular ways of seeing the world; and that none of us have a monopoly on wisdom or truth. (p. 59)

The fact that our understanding of the building is relational and perspectival only means that our understanding of the building is partial. To claim that our truths are objective—as is the norm—is a position that is simply theoretically untenable. This claim assumes that aperspectival views exist and also that an aperspectival view is a precondition of objectivity. But no view of the world or truth is ever aperspectival. Even if it were, no objectivity could be derived from such an assumption. Objectivity is relational: *It represents a relation to the world rather than a view of the world*. Objectivity represents any relation that strenuously strives to transcend the present. It is about being open to new truths. Subjectivity, on the other hand, represents a holding on to the present and the past. It represents an unwillingness to consider new truths. We find epistemological techniques that thwart the evolution of new truths. The other problem with our common conception of objectivity deals with the nature of the world and ourselves. We have long assumed that the world is constant, human beings are constant, and that both we and the world allow for constant understandings—that is, objectivity. Our popular understanding of objectivity assumes that the world is constant and fixed. It also fosters the belief that languages and techniques are completely transparent and have the ability to mirror the world. But as Evelyn Fox Keller (1995) explains:

> Confidence in the transparency of language in turn encourages the belief that one's own language is absolute. It permits the use of linguistic identifiers not only to define membership but also in support of an exclusionary understanding that secures the borders of scientific disciplines. Language, assumed to be transparent, becomes impervious. Closing the disciplinary borders against cross traffic serves to protect the indivisibility of all the inevitably self-reinforcing, even self-fulfilling, attributes of one's own language. The indifference of working scientists to (or their denial of) the self-enclosing nature of their language is no doubt helpful to the momentum of their research, but because it works to foreclose both internal awareness and external criticism of basic assumptions, it militates against deep-seated change. (p. 131)

Objectivity supposedly captures what *is*. However, what *is* is always unfolding and evolving. Objectivity resides within all the different perspectives of the building. A local truth can also be an objective truth. Objectivity is about viewing our *truths* as unfinished. It also means that the view of the building from which each truth emerges is open and seeks new understandings of the building. Objectivity is the quest to finish our *truths*.

Our common understanding of objectivity makes for domination because we use this understanding of objectivity to claim that our truths are the only truths. Objectivity allows us to mask our perspectivism—it prevents us from confronting the reality that our perspectivism reveals that other perspectives must also exist. Aperspectivism obliterates perspectivism. We brandish objectivity like a sword—cutting down any kind of truth that even hints of having any kind of cultural bias. On the other hand, our popular understandings of objectivity propagate assumptions that ultimately foster hegemony—such as, that a world exists outside of us that can be objectively mirrored, that objectivity means aperspectivism, and that perspectivism is bad. In this regard, objectivity allows for domination; it reflects our ambition to play gods. Objectivity presumes that human beings can attain a view of world that parallels that of gods. Perspectivism, on the other hand, tempers the power of our truths. It checks the domination that objectivity tends to foster. In this way, perspectivism fertilizes the ground for diversity and forces us to deal with the reality that our truths are partial and that other peoples can also make valid claims about the world. Both are humbling admissions. We are also forced to deal with the reality that the world will ultimately reject our techniques of domination. We will never be gods. As Pearce and Littlejohn (1997) explain:

> To have a philosophical conversation is to think deeply about our respective places in the world, to consider the bases of our systems of thought, and to discover both the powers and limits of the worldviews that make us who we are. To have a philosophical conversation is to realize the rational and cultural origins of our own categories and to discover the contexts from which our ideas stem. It is to understand that our actions and identities are tightly tied to our ways of thinking. To have a philosophical conversation is to look beyond surface differences to normally occult points of connection and the disjunction among the peoples of the world. A philosophical conversation, then, moves us beyond old patterns to a place in which we can explore common ideas and differing assumptions. (pp. 212-213)

Our striving for meaning creation organically forces us to move to other positions in or around the building. This movement is vital to developing deep and meaningful human relations. Such movement undercuts reification. In emergent understandings of system theory, this striving for meaning represents *final causation*. Final causation is the striving for life element found within all natural systems. This is the element that animates all systems. It is the telos element. Final causation is the striving that makes for evolution and transformation. According to Marion (1992), "Final causation projects forward into time. . . . Final causation, in pure or isolated form, generates behavior that is unbridled by social or physical constraint; it is a purposive pursuit. . . . It is the process of stretching the plane" (p. 168). Emergent understandings of system theory also posit a dialectical relation between *final* and *efficient* causations. The latter represents the element that fashions the direction of final causation. Rites and rituals, customs and traditions, and other cultural artifacts all fashion our striving for meaning. The well-being of the system is undercut when efficient causation blocks rather than facilitates final causation. This occurs when efficient causation begins to stress repetition rather than creation, thereby upsetting the natural harmony between both causations. The result is reification—the transfer of life to our creations so as to curb the momentum of final causation. The tendency to curb the momentum of final causation confronts us for a variety of compelling reasons.

Reification limits the anxiety that creation causes. Creation, after all, is entwined with destruction, and the evolution of new meanings leads to the devolution of other meanings. Creation demands that we confront the ambiguity of the world. It demands that we deal with the unknown and the lack of control and certainty, all of which bring anxiety. Reification also allows us to keep the ambiguity of the world to a minimum by circumscribing and delimiting human action. This narrowing also limits anxiety. In delimiting human action, reification also delimits volition and, consequently, responsibility. Reification limits our obligation and commitment to each other. It serves the politics and ethics of separation rather than union. Reification also thwarts diversity by encumbering the evolution of new and different ways of being. The point is that reification undercuts creation by thwarting our natural proclivity to develop new ways of being and understanding the world. It thwarts meaning creation. Further, reification undercuts transformation, disequilibrium, and discontinuity. It undercuts life. Most of all, reification blocks the formation of the deep and meaningful relations that flow from vibrant meaning creation processes. In *Developing Through Relationships*, Alan Fogel (1980) writes about how reification harms the evolution of such relations:

When relationships evolve into patterns in which participants perceive them as sequences of discrete exchanges or reward and cost it is quite likely that the creativity has gone out of them. They are no longer dynamic systems in which individuals grow, they have become prisons of the soul. Repeated encounters, therefore, can sometimes dull the senses and produce hatred, anger, and boredom. It is not mere repetition that leads to creative elaboration, it is one's stance toward the other, one's openness to change and desire to create new meaning through the relationship. (p. 90)

Fogel also writes that "Relationships must have . . . something not quite known, something that may never be understood or even articulated, something that entices the mind and body and that renews the meaning in the relationship" (p. 90). The undercutting of reification makes for a natural catalyst that propels us to different positions around the building. This natural catalyst, again, resides within all natural systems. Its ambition is to affirm life by allowing for evolution and transformation. The movement that the natural catalyst affords also exercises our capacity for empathy. Empathy is exercised by our willingness to suspend our original positions. In addition, empathy engenders trust, which is foundational to the forging of deep and meaningful human relations. Most of all, empathy nurtures union. It creates and sustains relationships. It lessens the threat of our differences. Accordingly, our proclivity for meaning creation organically nurtures our becoming fully human through the forging of deep and meaningful human relations. Our redemption resides within the blossoming of our proclivity and capacity to bring meaning to bear on the world.

Communication manifests our ability to help with the completion of the world. Without communication, various perspectives of the building will be absent and the world will be left unfinished. In turn, without those perspectives no catalyst exists to emblazon the existential and spiritual dimension of our humanity. Communication is both cultural and universal. It is cultural from the standpoint that meanings always reflect and belong to different perspectives of the building—meanings are perspectival and relational. On the other hand, communication is universal from the standpoint that meanings push against local perspectives. Communication both places and displaces us. It simultaneously gives us an understanding of the building and undercuts that understanding.

This reality is most evident when experiences are shared (reenacted). We can never mirror our experiences or our thoughts. Each retelling creates new experiences, new meanings, new understandings, and, often, even new truths. Communication enables us by affording us constant access to new experiences, new meanings, and so on. No meaning can be held constant. Consequently, no meaning can be transmitted.

Communication as transmission—a bedrock assumption of popular definitions of culture—wrongly assumes that human beings are passive to
the world. We are supposedly molded by prevailing discursive, communicative, and performative practices, simply the products of our genes or
our cultures. This makes for the stability and continuity that popular
definitions of culture reflect. Deetz (1995) correctly argues that to view
communication as transmission misses the politics of self construction. It
depoliticizes communication by masking issues of identity formation
and blocking scrutiny of the deep ideological structures that constrict
meaning creation processes. Deetz (1995) puts the matter aptly:

> Communication is about dialogic, collaborative constructions of self,
> other, and world in the process of making collective decisions. This
> includes the production and reproduction of personal identities,
> social knowledge, and social structures. From a communication per-
> spective, the political attention is to describe how the inner world,
> outer world, social relations, and means of expression are reciprocal-
> ly constituted with the interactional process as its own best explana-
> tion. In this sense, if psychological explanations explain individual
> behavior using goals, needs, and drives; and sociological explana-
> tions explain collective action using economic class difference, social
> structures, and forms of integration; communication explanations
> explain political practice by showing how goals, needs, drives, eco-
> nomic class, social structures, and forms of integration are produced
> and reproduced in interaction. (p. 107)

Deetz also argues that the notion of autonomous beings undercuts looking at communication ethically. He writes, "The fiction of fully
formed autonomous persons has important consequences for social and
political processes and for the way we do business. . . . If the person's
insides are independently formed, fully known, and without conflict,
only the granting of freedom is necessary for self-representation and full
participation in decision making. . . . [But] we must consider the politics
of self formation and interaction processes that aid in exploring one's self
and the construction thereof" (p. 61). Indeed, when communication is
seen as expression or transmission, this connotes autonomous beings and
this leaves uninterrogated the context that fashions all meaning creation
culturally, politically, and ethically. The result is that the status quo goes
uninterrogated and any possibility of new ways of being is undercut.
Consequently, when communication is reduced to expression or transmission, the possibility of diversity is severely undermined.

An existential and spiritual understanding of communication
reveals that human beings are recursively molded by the world. Besides
drawing our attention to the political element of the construction of self,

this understanding of communication also draws our attention to the existential and spiritual elements that undergird our relation to the world and each other. It deepens our understanding of what being human means. To look at communication as an existential and spiritual striving also deepens our understanding of diversity. Rather than simply being about differences, diversity reflects transformation and evolution. It represents the affirmation of life. It represents the end of communication practices that block disequilibrium, discontinuity, and diversity. Diversity is an artifact of deep and meaningful relations. It blossoms when our potentiality unfolds and our relations to each other deepen.

Nothing is fundamentally wrong with deep beliefs and convictions. The problem emerges when rigid structures—reflecting reification and deification—delimit our engagement with the world and each other, and, as a result, delimit the development of our humanity. The problem emerges when our beliefs and convictions are based on fear. Fear fosters stridency. It suppresses conflict and diversity. Accordingly, nothing about deep beliefs and convictions conflicts with empathy, compassion, transparency, and transformation.

To admit that no meaning can be owned changes our relation to the world. It undermines the potency of the ethos that human beings have the ability to exact control upon the world and each other through the transmission of meanings. As Ronald Arnett (1986) explains, "The taken-for-granted importance of possessing and having in Western culture discourages views of human communication that would reject possession of meaning" (p. 56). The fact that no meaning can be completely owned means that no meaning is ever final, ever certain. Meanings are always open to reinterpretation, elaboration, and, even, distortion. That this is the case means that human beings have to develop ways of being that are always open to negotiation. We have to develop ways of being that foster negotiation rather than transmission. Besides distorting our understanding of communication, the transmission metaphor distorts our understanding of human beings and the world. We have seen that it makes for a politics and ethics that thwart our existential and spiritual strivings. The transmission metaphor releases us of any obligation to other human beings. It puts the focus on symbols rather than relationships. It exaggerates our ability to control others through communication. This exaggeration is evident in popular definitions of culture. The assumption is that cultures spring from the transfer of signs, symbols, rituals, and so forth. We find an ethics of selfishness and self-centeredness. We find a fixation with our meanings and finding the best means to convey such meanings. In this regard, many peoples and cultures speak about instilling children with certain religious values and beliefs. It is assumed that our children are blank slates. No attention is given to what our children want or feel. We find a communication and pedagogy of domination (Freire, 1993).

A negotiational and relational approach to meaning makes for a different ethics and politics. Meanings reflect shared ownership—they belong to relationships rather than to persons. What belongs to us are the mechanisms that afford meaning creation. The focus is on the process of communication. We endeavor to develop new meanings rather than attempt to sustain present and old meanings. We are co-constructors of meaning. We endeavor to possess nothing as nothing can be really possessed. Our belief that our meanings can be owned gives rise to the ethos that human beings can make the world succumb to objective truths. It is assumed that human beings have the ability to transmit such truths. Supposedly, all truths are capturable—it is merely a matter of having the means to do so. This kind of ethos permeates our cultures as, after all, cultures are artifacts of communication. Consequently, cultures born of a transmission view of communication have a proclivity for ethnocentrism. It is believed that our cultures have the only objective view of the world. Our truths are the only truths, and our gods the only gods. The ethos of ownership permeates our cultures. With ownership comes the notion of protection. Our meanings and experiences have to be kept sacred. Eventually, different cultures clash, and the result, most often, is destruction. It would seem that this is a compelling enough reason to abandon a transmission view of communication.

A negotiational and relational view of communication views cultures in constant states of transformation and evolution. Rather than residing within language, meanings reside within our relationship to each other. Our truths, our view of the world, our conceptions of god, all belong to our relationship to the world and each other. Simply put, our truths and worldviews are all perspectival. This view assumes that other truths, other gods, and other views of the world are valid. It also assumes that no truth is ever finished, neither is any meaning ever closed to reinterpretation, elaboration, and even correction. It, however, by no means suggests that all truths are equally valid. On the other hand, what validity means is also relational.

Our proclivity and capacity for communication show us having other *business* with the world. Communication as an existential and spiritual striving locates human beings within an existential and spiritual world. An existential and spiritual understanding of communication also problematizes communication ethically and morally. In positing human beings as existential and spiritual, the corollary is that human beings are moral, and communication as a moral phenomenon demands certain ethical and moral obligations. Such obligations entail the engendering of trust, empathy, affirmation, openness, honesty, and compassion, ways of being that affirm life. The obligation pertains to the fostering of ways of being that allow us to become fully human through the forging of deep and meaningful human relations. As Chase (1993) nicely concludes, "The ultimate purpose of communication studies—from a spiritual perspective—should be to retrieve a sense of the Other through human interaction, to create human relationships which foster the call of the Other, not disguise it" (p. 15).

We are consumed with naming and labeling the world—forever checking and rechecking what our signs and symbols mean. We seem oblivious to the fact that only human beings and relationships have meaning. We are determined to sustain the illusion that the world can succumb to our techniques. Yet our claim to an unsurpassed progress is deeply suspect. We no longer burn people at stakes, nor are we deathly afraid to contest the authority of the establishment, but—without discounting the horrors and evils of the hegemony of religion—this progress must be seen against other aspects of modern society. The level of barbarism and human destruction that has occurred under the watch of the hegemony of the secular is unparalleled. It is also only modern society that can lay claim to possessing the means to bring real destruction upon the world. It is also only modern society that can claim the kind of environmental destruction that now perilously threatens an environmental armageddon. Our unparalleled levels of mental illness and human misery also point to a tenuous conception of progress. We seem bent on thwarting our existential and spiritual strivings. The result is human relations laden with distrust, fear, apathy, suspicion, and selfishness. The result is hierarchy and the end of diversity. We have spun our own webs of oppression. As Thayer (1973) observes:

> To be human is to be social. But the conditions of that sociation, because they feed off of as well as into human consciousness, will inevitably have consequences for the conditions of human existence. As manmade environments, within which people may live by the illusion of some necessary relationship between themselves and their environment, human societies will always bear upon the conditions of human existence. Like any of our artifacts, our societies may serve us well or ill. The burden of our hubris is that the responsibility for how our artifacts serve us belong not of them, but to us. (p. 133)

A valid concern is that any theory that stresses an ethos of evolution and transformation makes for nothing being sacred. Yet nothing is further from the truth. An ethos of evolution and transformation reveals a lot that is sacred. It reveals that this is a moral world and that human beings have a moral potentiality. It also reveals that human beings have a moral responsibility to exercise dialogical ways of being. An ethos of evolution and transformation affirms union rather than separation. What is sacred are ways of being that affirm the potential of the world. Our capacity and proclivity for meaning creation also shows human beings having a moral responsibility to the world. The nature of this responsibility resides within our existential and spiritual strivings. Finally, an ethos of evolution and transformation reveals that the world is laden with potentiality. It affirms the spiritual view that God has left to us the task to finish the world.

SUMMARY AND CONCLUSION

We need a new relation to the ambiguity of the world. Integral to any emergent relation must be the recognition that our proclivity and capacity for meaning construction is the means of bringing forth the potential of the world. Our proclivity and capacity for meaning creation also represents our means to help with the completion of the world. Our relation to the world is thus one of collaboration rather than subordination.

Attention to our universals in no way diminishes attention to the richness of our differences. Actually, such attention expands our understanding of differences by showing the common universals that fashion all cultures. Universals also release us from the belief that our differences damn us to conflict and war, and that our differences constrict our understanding to objectively understand the world. In fact, universals show our differences with the potentiality to expand our understanding of the world by committing us to ways of being that allow for the evolution of new differences. Such ways of being, besides fostering new differences, also foster union rather than separation. Universals also point to our common humanity. Universals show all human beings with the potentiality for union. In doing so, universals point to an ethos that transcends our differences. We do have a moral obligation, regardless of our differences, to treat others compassionately and tenderly. Finally, universals point to a sacred relation between us and the world. Our questing for communication, union, and evolution shows that our condition is entwined with that of the world. The responsibility for the condition of the world ultimately belongs to all of us.

Epilogue

The possibility of liberation resides within our proclivity and capacity to develop human relations woven with empathy, compassion, diversity, trust, equality, and love. It requires new conceptions of our humanity, our relation to each other, and the world. It also requires a broader definition of responsibility. The popular belief that people have been duped, and thus all that is required is theory, releases us of any responsibility for the condition of the world. A broader definition of responsibility assumes that the well-being of ourselves and others can only occur relationally. We need each other to attain liberation. We also need each other to construct *good* meaning. As Shulman (1996) observes, "If we do not cultivate our abilities to create and reconstruct meanings we will end up with a culture less sophisticated rather than more. On the other hand, if we take meaning to be a process in the human infrastructure, we are correctly placing the responsibility for meaning creation and manipulation in human hands, not mechanical ones" (p. 368).

To look at liberation secularly only cheapens what being human means. It emasculates community of all existential and spiritual virtues. It lessens our commitment to each other. Liberation requires us to own up to our responsibility to ourselves and each other to construct and sustain deep and meaningful human relations. It locates responsibility squarely within a moral context. Tying our own becoming with that of the world also expands our understanding of moral development. We have a moral responsibility to arrest our fear of our humanity, to affirm the humanity of others, to exercise empathy and compassion, and to aid the cultivation of deep and meaningful relations. In this way, the theory of liberation that this project offers is a moral theory.

I make bold claims about what being human means and the potential of human beings. I posit that only human relations that engender empathy, compassion, equality, and diversity are moral. I condemn any arrangement that legitimizes hierarchy and domination. I have sought to show that looking at diversity existentially and spiritually allows us to transcend what many view as hard moral decisions resulting from a supposedly unresolvable tension between diversity and unity. What contributes to this unnecessary tension is the belief that our only options to deal with differences are limited to assimilation or toleration. I have sought to release us from this decisional prism by reformulating our understanding of diversity. In locating the origins of diversity in union, I sought to show how the notions of union and separation expand our understanding of liberation. Liberation reveals a lot about our potential relation to the world. It reveals that creation rather than subordination is the path to realizing all that is good and sacred about the world. It entwines our being with the condition of the world.

Appendix A

RESOLUTION OF THE BOARD OF EDUCATION ADOPTING THE REPORT AND RECOMMENDATIONS OF THE AFRICAN-AMERICAN TASK FORCE; A POLICY STATEMENT AND DIRECTING THE SUPERINTENDENT OF SCHOOLS TO DEVISE A PROGRAM TO IMPROVE THE ENGLISH LANGUAGE ACQUISITION AND APPLICATION SKILLS OF AFRICAN-AMERICAN STUDENTS.

Whereas, numerous validated scholarly studies demonstrate that African American students as part of their culture and history as African people possess and utilize a language described in various scholarly approaches as "Ebonics" (literally Black sounds) or Pan African Communication Behaviors or African Language Systems; and

Whereas, these studies have also demonstrated that African Language Systems are genetically-based and not a dialect of English; and

Whereas, these studies demonstrate that such West and Niger-Congo African languages have been officially recognized and addressed in the mainstream public educational community as worth of study, understanding or application of its principles, laws and structures for the benefit of African American students both in terms of positive appreciation of the language and these students' acquisition and mastery of English language skills; and

Whereas, such recognition by scholars has given rise over the past 15 years to legislation passed by the State of California recognizing the unique language stature of descendants of slaves, with such legislation being prejudicially and unconstitutionally vetoed repeatedly by various California state governors; and

Whereas, judicial cases in states other than California have recognized the unique language stature of African American pupils, and such recognition by courts has resulted in court-mandated educational programs which have substantially benefitted African American children in the interest of vindicating their equal protection of the law rights under the 14th Amendment to the United States Constitution; and

Whereas, the Federal Bilingual Education Act (20 USC 1402 et seq.) mandates that local educational agencies "build their capacities to establish, implement and sustain programs of instruction for children and youth of limited English proficiency,'"; and

Whereas, the interests of the Oakland Unified School District in providing equal opportunities for all of its students dictate limited English proficient educational programs recognizing the English language acquisition and improvement skills of African American students are as fundamental as is application of bilingual education principles for others whose primary languages are other than English; and

Whereas, the standardized tests and grade scores of African American students in reading and language art skills measuring their application of English skills are substantially below state and national norms and that such deficiencies will be remedied by application of a program featuring African Language Systems principles in instructing African American children both in their primary language and in English; and

Whereas, standardized tests and grade scores will be remedied by application of a program with teachers and aides who are certified in the methodology of featuring African Language Systems principles in instructing African American children both in their primary language and in English. The certified teachers of these students will be provided incentives including, but not limited to salary differentials,

Now, therefore, be it resolved that the Board of Education officially recognizes the existence and the cultural and historic bases of West and Niger-Congo African Language Systems, and each language as the predominantly primary language of African American students; and

Be it further resolved that the Board of Education hereby adopts the report recommendations and attached Policy Statement of the District's

African American Task Force on language stature of African American speech; and

Be it further resolved that the Superintendent in conjunction with her staff shall immediately devise and implement the best possible academic program for imparting instruction to African American students in their primary language for the combined purposes of maintaining the legitimacy and richness of such language whether it is known as "Ebonics," "African Language Systems," "Pan African Communication Behaviors" or other description, and to facilitate their acquisition and mastery of English language skills; and

Be it further resolved that the Board of Education hereby commits to earmark District general and special funding as is reasonably necessary and appropriate to enable the Superintendent and her staff to accomplish the foregoing; and

Be it further resolved that the Superintendent and her staff shall utilize the input of the entire Oakland educational community as well as state and federal scholarly and educational input in devising such a program; and

Be it further resolved, that periodic reports on the progress of the creation and implementation of such an educational program shall be made to the Board of Education at least once per month commencing at the Board meeting of December 18, 1996.

POLICY STATEMENT

There is persuasive empirical evidence that, predicated on analysis of the phonology, morphology and syntax that currently exists as systematic, rule governed and predictable patterns exist in the grammar of African-American speech. The validated and persuasive linguistic evidence is that African-Americans (1) have retained a West and Niger-Congo African linguistic structure in the substratum of their speech and (2) by this criteria are not native speakers of black dialect or any other dialect of English.

Moreover, there is persuasive empirical evidence that, owing to their history as United States slave descendants of West and Niger-Congo African origin, to the extent that African-Americans have been born into, reared in, and continue to live in linguistic environments that are different from the Euro-American English speaking population, African-American people and their children, are from home environments in which a language other than English language is dominant within the meaning of "environment where a Language other than English is dominant" as defined in Public Law 1-13-382 (20 U.S.C. 7402, et seq.).

The policy of the Oakland Unified School District (OUSD) is that all pupils are equal and are to be treated equally. Hence, all pupils who have difficulty speaking, reading, writing or understanding the English language and whose difficulties may deny to them the opportunity to learn successfully in classrooms where the language of instruction is English or to participate fully in classrooms where the language of instruction is English or to participate fully in our society are to be treated equally regardless of their race or national origin.

As in the case of Asian-American, Latino-American, Native American and all other pupils in this District who come from backgrounds or environments where a language other than English is dominant, African-American pupils shall not, because of their race, be subtly dehumanized, stigmatized, discriminated against or denied. Asian-American, Latino-American, Native American and all other language different children are provided general funds for bilingual education, English as Second Language (ESL) and State and Federal (Title VIII) Bilingual education programs to address their limited and non-English proficient (LEP/NEP) needs. African-American pupils are equally entitled to be tested and, where appropriate, shall be provided general funds and State and Federal (Title VIII) bilingual education and ESL programs to specifically address their LEP/NEP needs.

All classroom teachers and aids who are bilingual in Nigritian Ebonics (African-American Language) and English shall be given the same salary differentials and merit increases that are provided to teachers of the non-African American LEP pupils in the OUSD.

With a view toward assuring that parents of African-American pupils are given the knowledge base necessary to make informed choices, it shall be the policy of the Oakland Unified School District that all parents of LEP (Limited English Proficient) pupils are to be provided the opportunity to partake of any and all language and culture specific teacher education and training classes designed to address their child's LEP needs.

On all home language surveys given to parents of pupils requesting home language identification or designations, a description of the District's programmatic consequences of their choices will be contained.

Nothing in this Policy shall preclude or prevent African-American parents who view their child's limited English proficiency as being non-standard English, as opposed to being West and Niger-Congo African Language based, from exercising their right to choose and to have their child's speech disorders and English Language deficits addressed by special education and/or other District programs.

Appendix B

AMENDED
RESOLUTION OF THE
BOARD OF EDUCATION
ADOPTING THE REPORT AND RECOMMENDATIONS
OF THE AFRICAN-AMERICAN TASK FORCE;
A POLICY STATEMENT
AND
DIRECTING THE SUPERINTENDENT OF SCHOOLS
TO DEVISE A PROGRAM TO IMPROVE THE
ENGLISH LANGUAGE ACQUISITION AND APPLICATION
SKILLS
OF AFRICAN-AMERICAN STUDENTS

WHEREAS, numerous validated scholarly studies demonstrate that African-American students as a part of their culture and history **as** African people possess and utilize a language described in various scholarly approaches as "Ebonics" (literally "Black sounds") or "Pan African Communication Behaviors" or "African Language Systems"; and

WHEREAS, these studies have also demonstrated that African Language Systems **have origins in West and Niger-Congo languages** and **are** not **merely** dialects of English; and

WHEREAS, these studies demonstrate that such West and Niger-Congo African languages have been recognized and addressed in the educational community as worthy of study, understanding **and** application of their principles, laws and structures for the benefit of African-American students both in terms of positive appreciation of the language and these students' acquisition and mastery of English language skills; and

WHEREAS, such recognition by scholars has given rise over the past fifteen years to legislation passed by the State of California recognizing the unique language stature of descendants of slaves, with such legislation being prejudicially and unconstitutionally vetoed repeatedly by various California state governors; and

WHEREAS, judicial cases in states other than California have recognized the unique language stature of African American pupils, and such recognition by courts has resulted in court-mandated educational programs which have substantially benefited African-American children in the interest of vindicating their equal protection of the law rights under the Fourteenth Amendment to the United States Constitution; and

WHEREAS, the Federal Bilingual Education Act (20 U.S.C. 1402 et seq.) mandates that local educational agencies "build their capacities to establish, implement and sustain programs of instruction for children and youth of limited English proficiency"; and

WHEREAS, the interest of the Oakland Unified School District in providing equal opportunities for all of its students dictate limited English proficient educational programs recognizing the English language acquisition and improvement skills of African-American students are as fundamental as is application of bilingual or **second language learner** principles for others whose primary languages are other than English. **Primary languages are the language patterns children bring to school;** and

WHEREAS, the standardized tests and grade scores of African-American students in reading and language arts skills measuring their application of English skills are substantially below state and national norms and that such deficiencies will be remedied by application of a program featuring African Language Systems principles **to move students from the language patterns they bring to school to English proficiency;** and

WHEREAS, standardized tests and grade scores will be remedied by application of a program that teachers and **instructional assistants,** who are certified in the methodology of African Language Systems principles

used to transition students from the language patterns they bring to school to English. The certified teachers of these students will be provided incentives including, but not limited to salary differentials;

NOW, THEREFORE, BE IT RESOLVED that the Board of Education officially recognizes the existence, and the cultural and historic bases of West and Niger-Congo African Language Systems, and each language as the primary language of **many** African-American students; and

BE IT FURTHER RESOLVED that the Board of Education hereby adopts the report, recommendations and attached Policy Statement of the District's African-American Task Force on **the** language stature of African-American speech; and

BE IT FURTHER RESOLVED that the Superintendent in conjunction with her staff shall immediately devise and implement the best possible academic program for the combined purposes of facilitating **the acquisition and mastery of English language skills, while respecting and embracing** the legitimacy and richness of the language *patterns* whether **they are** known as "Ebonics", "African Language Systems", "Pan African Communication Behaviors", or other description; and

BE IT FURTHER RESOLVED that the Board of Education hereby commits to earmark District general and special funding as is reasonably necessary and appropriate to enable the Superintendent and her staff to accomplish the foregoing; and

BE IT FURTHER RESOLVED that the Superintendent and her staff shall utilize the input of the entire Oakland educational community as well as state and federal scholarly and educational input in devising such a program; and

BE IT FURTHER RESOLVED that periodic reports on the progress of the creation and implementation of such an educational program shall be made to the Board of Education at least once per month commencing at the Board meeting of December 18, 1996.

References

Abelson, R. (1999, July 14). Study finds diversity programs ineffective at getting women minorities to the top. *New York Times*, p. B3.

Aiello, L. C. (1998). The foundations of language. In N. G. Jablonski & L. C. Aiello (Eds.), *The origins and diversification of language* (pp. 21-34). San Francisco: California Academy of Sciences.

Allen, B. J. (1995). "Diversity" and organizational communication. *Journal of Applied Communication Research, 23,* 143-155.

Allen, B. J. (1996). Feminist standpoint theory: A black woman's (re)view of organizational socialization. *Communication Studies, 47,* 257-271.

Allen, B. J. (1998). Black womanhood and feminist standpoints. *Management Communication Quarterly, 11,* 575-586.

Allen, B. J., Orbe, M. P., & Refugia, M. (1999). The complexity of our tears: Dis/enchantment and (in)difference in the academy. *Communication Theory, 9,* 402-429.

Aoki, K. (1991). Some theoretical aspects of the origin of cultural transmission. In S. Osawa & T. Honjo (Eds.), *Evolution of life: Fossils, molecules, and culture* (pp. 439-452). New York: Springer-Verlag.

Arnett, R. C. (1986). *Communication and community*. Carbondale: Southern Illinois Press.

Axelrod, R. (1984). *The evolution of cooperation*. New York: Basic Books.

Baldwin, J. (1997). If black English isn't a language, then tell me, what is? *Black Scholar, 27*, 5-6.

Barker, J. R. (1993). Tightening the iron cage: Concertive control in self-managing teams. *Administrative Science Quarterly, 38*, 408-437.

Bergman, S. H. (1991). *Dialogical philosophy from Kierkegaard to Buber*. Albany: State University of New York Press.

Bernstein, R. (1994). *Dictatorship of virtue*. New York: Knopf.

Bickerton, D. (1995). *Language and human behavior*. Seattle: University of Washington Press.

Bloom, A. (1987). *The closing of the American mind*. New York: Simon & Schuster.

Bohm, D. (1980). *Wholeness and the implicate order*. New York: Routledge.

Bookchin, M. (1995). *Re-enchanting humanity*. New York: Cassell.

Bork, R. H. (1996). *Slouching towards Gomorrah*. New York: Regan Books.

Bowen, J. R. (1996). The myth of global ethnic conflict. *Journal of Democracy, 7*, 3-14.

Boyd, D. (1996). Dominance concealed through diversity: Implications of inadequate perspectives on cultural pluralism. *Harvard Educational Review, 66*, 609-630.

Brimelow, P. (1995). *Alien nation*. New York: Random House.

Bryant, C. (1985). *Positivism in social research*. New York: St. Martin's Press.

Buber, M. (1970). *I and thou* (W. Kaufman, Trans.). New York: Scribner's Sons.

Buber, M. (1994). Genuine dialogue and the possibilities of peace. In R. Anderson, K. Cissna, & R. Arnett (Eds.), *The reach of dialogue: Confirmation, voice, and community* (pp. 306-312). Cresskill, NJ: Hampton Press.

Buzzanell, P. (1994). Gaining a voice: Feminist organizational communication theorizing. *Management Communication Quarterly, 7*, 339-383.

Buzzanell, P. (1995). Reframing the glass ceiling as a socially constructed process. Implications for understanding and change. *Communication Monographs, 62*, 327-354.

Buzzanell, P. (1999). Tensions and burdens in employment interviewing processes: Perspectives of non-dominant group applicants. *Journal of Business Communication, 36*, 134-162.

Chase, K. R. (1993). A spiritual and critical revision of structuration theory. *Journal of Communication and Religion, 16*, 1-21.

Cherwitz, R. A., & Hikins, J. W. (1990). Irreducible dualisms and the residue of commonsense: On the inevitability of Cartesian anxiety. *Philosophy and Rhetoric, 23*, 229-241.

Cherwtiz, R. A., & Darwin, T. J. (1995). Toward a relational theory of meaning. *Philosophy and Rhetoric, 28*, 17-29.

Chomsky, N. (1968). *Language and mind*. New York: Harcourt.

Cissna, K. N., & Anderson, R. (1994). Communication and the ground of dialogue. In R. Anderson, K. Cissna, & R. Arnett (Eds.), *The reach of dialogue* (pp. 9-30). Cresskill, NJ: Hampton Press.

Clair, R. P. (1998). *Organizing silence: A world of possibilities*. Albany: State University of New York Press.

Clegg, R. C. (1989). *Frameworks of power*. Newbury Park, CA: Sage.

Cohen, M. N. (1998, April 17). Culture, not race, explain human diversity. *The Chronicle of Higher Education*, pp. B4-B5.

Cohen, J., Howard, M., & Nussbaum, M. C. (Eds.). (1999). *Is multiculturalism bad for women?* Princeton, NJ: Princeton University Press.

Collins, P. H. (1991). *Black feminist thought: Knowledge, consciousness, and the politics of empowerment*. New York: Routledge.

Colt, G. H. (1997, August). The magic of touch. *Life*, pp. 53-62.

Dawkins, R. (1989). *The selfish gene*. Oxford: Oxford University Press.

Deetz, S. (1995). *Transforming communication, transforming business*. Cresskill, NJ: Hampton Press.

Dennett, D. C. (1995). *Darwin's dangerous idea*. New York: Touchstone.

Dervin, B. (1980). Communication gaps and inequities: Moving toward a reconceptualization. In B. Dervin & M. J. Voight (Eds.), *Progress in communication sciences* (Vol. 2, pp. 73-112). Norwood, NJ: Ablex.

Dervin, B. (1991). Comparative theory reconceptualized: From entities and states to processes and dynamics. *Communication Theory, 1*, 59-69.

Devine, P. E. (1996). *Human diversity and the culture wars*. Westport, CT: Praeger.

De Wahl, F. B. M. (1999, June 17). Cultural primacy comes of age. *Nature*, pp. 635-636.

Downs, A. (1998). The big picture: How American cities are growing. *Brookings Review, 16*, 8-11.

D'Souza, D. (1995). *The end of racism*. New York: The Free Press.

Ellul, J. (1994). Seeing and hearing: Prolegomena. In R. Anderson, K. Cissna, & R. Arnett (Eds.), *The reach of dialogue: Confirmation, voice, and community* (pp. 120-125). Cresskill, NJ: Hampton Press.

Etzioni, A. (1996, September). From melting pot to mosaic. *Current*, pp. 8-13.

Fairbanks, S. (1999). Suburban sprawl. *Amicus Journal, 21*, 15.

Farber, D. A., & Sherry, S. (1997). *Beyond all reason*. New York: Oxford University Press.

Feuer, L. S., (1991). From pluralism to multiculturalism. *Society, 21*, 19-22.

Field, T. M. (1998, December). Massage therapy effects. *American Psychologist*, pp. 1270-1281.

Fish, S. (1989). *Doing what comes naturally: Change, rhetoric, and practice of theory in literary and legal studies.* Durham, NC: Duke University Press.

Fish, S. (1997). Boutique multiculturalism, or why liberals are incapable of thinking about hate speech. *Critical Inquiry, 23,* 378-395.

Fogel, A. (1993). *Developing through relationships.* Chicago: University of Chicago Press.

Fotion, N., & Elfstrom, G. (1992). *Toleration.* Tuscaloosa University of Alabama Press.

Fowers, B. J., & Richardson, F. C. (1996). Why is multiculturalism good? *American Psychologist, 51,* 609-621.

Freire, P. (1993). *Pedagogy of the oppressed.* New York: Continuum.

Fromm, E. (1956). *The art of loving.* New York: Harper & Row.

Fromm, E. (1973). *The anatomy of human destructiveness.* New York: Henry Holt.

Furbank, P. N. (1997). On pluralism. *Raritan, 17,* 83-95.

Garner, T. (1994). Oral rhetorical practice in African American culture. In A. Gonzalez, M. Houston, & V. Chen (Eds.), *Our voices: Essays in culture, ethnicity, and communication* (pp. 81-91). Los Angeles: Roxbury.

Gersh, J. (1996). Subdivide and conquer. *Amicus Journal, 18,* 14-20.

Glazer, N. (1997). *We are all multiculturalists now.* Cambridge, MA: Harvard University Press.

Gleason, P. (1992). *Speaking of diversity.* Baltimore, MD: John Hopkins University Press.

Gonzalez, M. C. (1998). Abandoning the sacred hierarchy: Disempowering hegemony through spirit. In M. Hecht (Ed.), *Communicating prejudice* (pp. 223-234). Newbury Park, CA: Sage.

Goodall, H. L., Jr. (1993). Mysteries of the future told: Communication as the material manifestation of spirituality. *World Communication Journal, 22,* 40-49.

Gould, S. J. (1999, July 2). The human difference. *The New York Times,* p. A8.

Gudykunst, W. B., & Hammer, M. R. (1988). The influence of social identity and intimacy of interethnic relationships on uncertainty reduction processes. *Human Communication Research, 14,* 569-601.

Haney Lopez, I. F. (1996). *White by law: The legal construction of race.* New York: New York University Press.

Haviland, W. A. (1993). *Cultural anthropology.* Fort Worth, TX: Harcourt, Brace, Jovanovich.

Huntington, S. P. (1996a, November/December). The West: Unique, not universal. *Foreign Affairs,* pp. 28-46.

Huntington, S. P. (1996b). *The clash of civilizations and the remaking of world order.* New York: Simon & Schuster.

Hurford, J. R., Studdert-Kennedy, M., & Knight, C. (Eds.). (1998). *Approaches to the evolution of language.* Cambridge, UK: Cambridge University Press.

Jourard, S. M. (1971). *The transparent self.* New York: Van Nostrand.

Kachru, B. B. (1999, April). *World Englishes and culture wars.* Paper presented at Purdue University, West Lafayette, IN.

Kallen, H. (1915, February). Democracy versus the melting pot. *Nation,* pp. 190-194.

Keller, E. F. (1995). *Reflections on gender and science.* New Haven, CT: Yale University Press.

Kennedy, R. (1995). The phony war. In S. Fraser (Ed.), *The bell curve wars* (pp. 179-186). New York: Basic Books.

Kimball, R. (1991, January 6). Tenured radicals: A postscript. *The New Criterion,* p. 6.

Kirkwood, W. B. (1993). Studying communication about spirituality and the spiritual consequences of communication. *Journal of Communication and Religion, 17,* 13-26.

Klein, M. (1997). Multiculturalism and its discontents. *New England Review, 18,* 75-80.

Knight, C. (1998). Introduction: Grounding language function in social cognition. In J. R. Hurford, M. Studdert-Kennedy, & C. Knight (Eds.), *Approaches to the evolution of language* (pp. 9-16). Cambridge, UK: Cambridge University Press.

Kochman, T. (1990). Force fields in black and white communication. In D. Carbaugh (Ed.), *Cultural communication and intercultural contact* (pp. 193-218). Hillsdale, NJ: Erlbaum.

Ladson-Billings, G. (1992). The multicultural mission: Unity and diversity. *Social Education, 56,* 308-311.

Lee, D. (1987). *Freedom and culture.* Prospects Heights, IL: Waveland Press.

Legutko, R. (1994). The trouble with toleration. *Partisan Review, 61,* 610-623.

Leinberger, C. (1998). The market and metropolitanism. *Brookings Review, 16,* 35-36.

Lightfoot, D. (1999). *The development of language.* Malden, MA: Blackwell.

Lincoln, Y., & Guba, E. (1985). *Naturalistic inquiry.* Beverly Hills, CA: Sage.

Linguistic Society of America (1997, January). *Resolution on the Oakland "ebonics" issue.* Chicago: Author.

Lippi-Green, R. (1997). *English with an accent: Language, ideology, and discrimination in the United States.* New York: Routledge.

Locke, J. L. (1998). Social sound-making as a precursor to spoken language. In J. R. Hurford, M. Studdert-Kennedy, & C. Knight (Eds.),

Approaches to the evolution of language (pp. 190-201). Cambridge, UK: Cambridge University Press.

Long, K. L. (1997, November). *Sparring with spirituality: Issues of entangling spirituality and communication.* Paper presented at the annual conference of the National Communication Association, Chicago, IL.

Longman, P. J. (1998, April 27). Who pays for sprawl? *U.S. News & World Report*, p. 22.

Lorde, A. (1984). *Sister outsider: Essays and speeches.* Trumansburg, NY: Crossing Press.

Marion, R. (1992). Chaos, topology, and social organization. *Journal of School Leadership, 2*, 144-178.

McCrone, J. (1991). *The ape that spoke: Language and the evolution of the human mind.* New York: William Morrow.

McPhail, M. L. (1996). Spirituality and the critique of epistemic rhetoric: A coherent analysis. *Journal of Communication and Religion, 19*, 48-60.

Miller, J. J. (1998). *The unmaking of Americans.* New York: The Free Press.

Milliken, F. J., & Martins, L. L. (1996). Searching for common threads: Understanding the multiple effects of diversity in organizational groups. *Academy of Management Review, 21*, 402-423.

Morin, R., & Balz, D. (1996, January 28). Americans losing trust in each other and institutions. *The Washington Post*, pp. A1, A6.

Mortensen, C. D. (1991). Communication, conflict, and culture. *Communication Theory, 4*, 273-293.

Mumby, D. K. (1988). *Communication and power in organizations: Discourse, ideology and domination.* Norwood, NJ: Ablex.

Neuliep, J. W. (1995). A comparison of teacher immediacy in African-American and Euro-Americans college classrooms. *Communication Education, 44*, 267-277.

Norton, D. L. (1991). *Democracy and moral development.* Berkeley: University of California Press.

Ohlhauser, J. B. (1996). Human rhetoric: Accounting for spiritual intervention. *Howard Journal of Communications, 7*, 339-348.

O'Keefe, D. (1994). Multiculturalism and cultural literacy. *The International Journal of Social Education, 9*, 66-80.

Ong, W. J. (1967). *Presence of the word.* Minneapolis: University of Minnesota Press.

Ong, W. J. (1981). *Fighting for life: Contest, sexuality, and consciousness.* Ithaca, NY: Cornell University Press.

Ong, W. J. (1982). *Orality and literacy: The technologizing of the word.* New York: Methuen.

Orbe, M. P. (1998). An outsider within perspective to organizational communication: Explicating the communicative practices of co-cultural group members. *Management Communication Quarterly, 12,* 230-279.

Pearce, W. B., & Littlejohn, S. W. (1997). *Moral conflict: When social worlds collide.* Thousands Oaks, CA: Sage.

Pease, D. E. (1997). Regulating multi-ahoccerists, Fish('s) rules. *Critical Inquiry, 23,* 396-418.

Peirce, N. R. (1995). The human cost of urban out-migration. *National Journal, 27,* 1297.

Phillips, A. (1997, Winter). Who's afraid of multiculturalism? *Dissent,* pp. 57-63.

Pinker, S. (1994). *The language instinct.* New York: HarperCollins.

Pokora, R. (1996). *And Mary danced: Communication and spirituality at a women's religious organization.* Unpublished doctoral dissertation, Purdue University, West Lafayette, IN.

Poulson, D. (1997, June 20). Religious groups focus: Suburban sprawl. *National Catholic Reporter,* p. 10.

Premack, A. J., & Premack, D. (1991). Teaching language to an ape. In William S-Y. Wang (Ed.), *The emergence of language development and evolution* (pp. 16-27). New York: W. H. Freeman.

Ravitch, D. (1990, October 24). Multiculturalism yes, particularism no. *The Chronicle of Higher Education,* p. A44.

Reinharz, S. (1988). Feminist distrust: Problems of content and content in sociological work. In D.N. Berg & K.K. Smith (Eds.), *The self in social inquiry* (pp. 122-153). Beverly Hills, CA: Sage.

Rodriguez, A. (2000). *On matters of liberation I: The case against hierarchy.* Cresskill, NJ: Hampton Press.

Rogers, C. R., (1980). *A way of being.* Boston: Houghton Mifflin.

Roth, B. M. (1994). *Prescription for failure: Race relations in the age of social science.* London: Transaction.

Rousseau, J. J. (1986). *The first and second discourses and essays on the origins of language.* New York: Harper & Row.

Sahlins, M. (1976). *The use and abuse of biology: An anthropological critique of sociobiology.* Ann Arbor: The University of Michigan Press.

Salins, P. D. (1997). *Assimilation American style.* New York: Basic Books.

Scanlon, T. M. (1996). The difficulty of tolerance. In D. Heyd (Ed.), *Toleration* (pp. 226-240). Princeton, NJ: Princeton University Press.

Schein, E. H. (1985). *Organizational culture and leadership.* San Francisco: Jossey-Bass.

Schlesinger, A. M. (1992). *The disuniting of America.* New York: W. W. Norton.

Schmidt, A. J. (1997). *The menace of multiculturalism: Trojan horse in America.* Westport, CT: Praeger.

Shulman, A. D. (1996). Putting group information technology in its place: Communication and good group performance. In S. R. Clegg, C. Hardy, & W. R. Nord (Eds.), *Handbook of organization studies* (pp. 357-374). London: Sage.

Smith, C. R. (1993). Finding the spiritual dimension of rhetoric. *Western Journal of Communication, 57,* 266-271.

Steele, S. (1998). *A dream deferred: The second betrayal of black freedom in America.* New York: HarperCollins.

Stohl, C., & Sotirin, P. (1989). Absence as workplace control: A critical inquiry. In J. Anderson (Ed.), *Communication Yearbook 13* (pp. 57-67). Newbury Park, CA: Sage.

Studdert-Kennedy, M., Knight, C., & Hurford, J. R. (1998). Introduction: New approaches to language evolution. In J. R. Hurford, M. Studdert-Kennedy, & C. Knight (Eds.), *Approaches to the evolution of language* (pp. 3-5). Cambridge, UK: Cambridge University Press.

Taylor, C. (1994). The politics of recognition. In A. Gutmann (Ed.), *Multiculturalism* (pp. 25-74). Princeton, NJ: Princeton University Press.

Thomas, C. (1998, July 20). Modern multiculturalism divides us. *The Dallas Morning News,* p. A11.

Thayer, L. (1997). *Pieces: Toward a revisioning of communication/life.* Greenwich, CT: Ablex.

Tompkins, P., & Cheney, G. (1983). Account analysis of organizations: Decision making and identification. In L. Putnam & M. Pacanowsky (Eds.), *Communication and organizations* (pp. 123-146). Beverly Hills, CA: Sage.

Torrance, R. M. (1994). *The spiritual quest.* Berkeley: University of California Press.

Turkey, D. (1990). Toward a research agenda for spiritual rhetoric. *Journal of Communication and Religion, 13,* 66-76.

Turner, F. (1996, March/April). Book review. *Society,* pp. 89-90.

Ulbaek, I. (1998). The origin of language and cognition. In J. R. Hurford, M. Studdert-Kennedy, & C. Knight (Eds.), *Approaches to the evolution of language* (pp. 30-43). Cambridge, UK: Cambridge University Press.

Von Humbolt, W. (1988). *On language.* New York: Cambridge University Press.

Wagner, G. W., Pfeffer, J., & O'Reilly, C. A. (9184). Organizational demography and turnover in top-management groups. *Academy of Management Review, 21,* 402-423.

Walzer, M. (1997). *On toleration.* New Haven, CT: Yale University Press.

Watson W. E., Kumar, K., & Michaelson, L. K. (1993). Cultural diversity's impact on interaction and performance: Comparing homogenous and diverse task groups. *Academy of Management Journal, 36,* 590-602.

Weissberg, R. (1998). *Political tolerance.* Thousand Oaks, CA: Sage.

Wen, H. (1999, March). Suburban renewal. *Texas Monthly,* pp. 66-77.

Whiten, A, Goodall, J., McGrew, W. C., Nishida, T., Reynolds, V., Sugiyama, Y., Tutin, C. E. G., Wrangham, R. W., & Boesch, C. (1999, June 17). Cultures in chimpanzees. *Nature,* pp. 682-685.

Whitfield, S. J. (1996). The mystique of multiculturalism. *The Virginia Quarterly Review, 72,* 429-445.

Wilson, E. O. (1978). *On human nature.* Cambridge, MA: Harvard University Press.

Witmer, D. F. (1997, November). *The co-construction of self and organization: Evoking organizational spirituality.* Paper presented at the annual conference of the National Communication Association, Chicago, IL.

Williamson, C. (1996). *The immigration mystique.* New York: Basic Books.

Worden, R. (1998). The evolution of language from social intelligence. In M. Studdert-Kennedy, C. Knight, & J. R. Hurford (Eds.), *Approaches to the evolution of language.* Cambridge, UK: Cambridge University Press.

Wright, R. (1999, November 8). We invite the hostages to return. *New Yorker,* pp. 38-47.

Zavarzadeh, M., & Morton, D. (1994). *Theory as resistance: Politics and culture after (post)structuralism.* New York: Guilford.

Author Index

Subject Index

163